# On the Abyss

The book is an attempt to understand the enormity of the crisis facing Pakistan. Will Gen. Pervez Musharraf be able to save his country from economic ruin, control corruption, curb the fundamentalists, keep the army happy and yet make peace with India? As the essayists point out, all that is highly unlikely. But the really frightening prospect for many people in Pakistan is that if Musharraf fails, the alternative is worse — the fundamentalists are waiting to take over.

The aim of the book is not to gloat over Pakistan's problems, but to understand them. For that reason, six of the eleven essays in the book are by eminent Pakistanis themselves. They take a long, hard, critical — and often despairing — look at their own country. They paint a bleak, gloomy picture but then, Pakistan is beset with problems, and many people there see Musharraf's military rule as the country's last chance to set things right. The Pakistani contributors include the London-based writer Tariq Ali, whose 1983 book, *Can Pakistan Survive — The Death of a State*, was a classic.

Providing the outsider's view in the book — since Indians and Pakistanis tend to have set views about each other — are three hard-nosed foreign correspondents in South Asia: Pamela Constable of the *Washington Post*, Jason Burke of the *Observer*, London, and Daniel Lak of the BBC. There are also two Indian contributors — Sankarshan Thakur of the *Telegraph*, who has covered elections in Pakistan; and the irrepressible Mani Shankar Aiyar, who was India's first consul-general in Karachi.

# On the Abyss

PAKISTAN AFTER THE COUP

HarperCollins *Publishers* India

HarperCollins *Publishers* India Pvt Ltd
7/16 Ansari Road, Daryaganj, New Delhi 110 002

First published in 2000 by
HarperCollins *Publishers* India

ISBN 81-7223-389-2

Photo credits:
Karen Davies on pages 1, 5, 6, 20, 27, 33, 39, 45, 57, 63, 79, 81, 84,
107, 114, 116, 139, 149, 157 and 226
Dieter Ludwig on pages 127, 158, 175 and 193
Associated Press on pages 13, 16, 24 and 75
Pamela Constable on pages 2, 95 and 167
Nirad Grover on pages 9 and 38
Indian Express on page 244
Jagdish Yadav on page 90

Typeset by
Nikita Overseas Pvt Ltd
19A Ansari Road
New Delhi 110 002

Printed in India by
Gopsons Papers Ltd
A-14 Sector 60
Noida 201 301

# Contents

# From the Publisher

*On the Abyss — Pakistan After the Coup* is the second in a new series launched by HarperCollins India called Contemporary Essays. We are much encouraged by the popular and critical success of our first book in this format, *Guns and Yellow Roses — Essays on the Kargil War*. In Contemporary Essays, we shall take an in-depth look at events and trends of recent importance — from major news events to social trends and popular culture. Whatever subject we choose, the attempt will be to rise above, and go beyond, what appears in the print and electronic media; to step outside the hype, and tell it like it is — warts and all. Each title will have essays by eminent writers and experts, and will include high quality pictures. We hope that readers will continue to appreciate our efforts and help us sustain the very attractive art of the essay.

# Acknowledgments

The Publishers would like to thank all the contributors for writing the essays at a short notice. We are particularly grateful to the writers from Pakistan for their trust and patience. The book would not have been possible without the enormous contribution of photographer Karen Davies in Islamabad, who gamely and graciously met our demands for more and more pictures. We would also like to thank Najam Sethi, editor of *Friday Times* in Lahore, who went out of his way to organise pictures for us; Dieter Ludwig for contributing his pictures; and Arthur Max, the South Asia bureau chief of the Associated Press in Delhi, for making archive pictures available. Thanks also to Pamela Constable for giving us her pictures and for her enthusiastic participation and to Sankarshan Thakur for his help and support right through the project.

# In the Doghouse

## TARIQ ALI

The London-based writer on the enormity of the tasks facing General Musharraf, and how a EU-style confederation of South Asian Republics could be a solution to Pakistan's problems.

*A general who has seized power via a putsch and aroused mass expectations, but ends up creating even more problems, could pave the way to further chaos.*

Pakistan is in the throes of a new crisis and the stakes, as always, are high. The moth-eaten democracy has been swiftly truncated. A new military regime has constructed a civilian charade around itself and think-tanks are flourishing, just like the poppy fields producing heroin under Taliban supervision next door. Will the new strongman, Gen. Pervez Musharraf, be able to modernise the country and its economy? Will he be able to disarm the fundamentalist groups without disturbing the equilibrium of the army? Will he be able to end the corruption and violence that has plagued all the major cities? And will he be able to make peace with India? To pose these questions is to stress the enormity of the tasks that face the general. A politician with a popular mandate and military support could accomplish these tasks, though the transition could not be painless. A general who has seized power via a putsch and aroused mass expectations, but ends up creating even more problems, could pave the way to further chaos.

Ever since its foundation in 1947, the Pakistani state has been plagued by a failure to establish strong democratic institutions. The reason is simple. From 1951 onwards, when the country had become a US pawn in the Cold War, Washington felt that the army was the best guarantor of its interests in the region. Gen. Ayub Khan's dictatorship (1958-69) was openly backed by the US state department, till it was swept aside by a popular uprising that lasted three months. Gen. Zia ul-Haq's monstrous regime (1977-1988) was spawned by the Pentagon and the Defence Intelligence Agency, eager for a proxy to take on the Russians in Afghanistan.

For the third time in its traumatic history, the army has seized power, and this time, apparently, against the advice of the US. The people — disillusioned, apathetic, weary — appear indifferent to the fate of their venal politicians. There is widespread disgust at the inability of successive governments to control the scale of corruption.

For several years now, the decay at the heart of the administration had become a national scandal. Politicians were so busy lining their own pockets that they had little time to ponder the welfare of the country and its people.

In 1997, a palace coup, orchestrated by her own handpicked president, removed Benazir Bhutto. It was alleged that she and her husband, Senator Asif Zardari, had used the Prime Minister's House to amass a large private fortune, estimated at somewhere close to one billion dollars.

In the subsequent general elections, her long-time opponent, Nawaz Sharif, scored a sensational triumph, winning eighty per cent of the seats in parliament, but on the basis of an exceptionally low turn-out. Only twenty-five per cent of the electorate bothered to vote. Benazir's supporters punished her by staying at home. The new government had promised a great deal, but nothing changed. The country continued to rot. Pakistan has never been able to provide the bulk of its population with either free education or health, but in the past it could offer food to the poor at subsidised prices and protect innocent lives from random killings. No longer. Everything is falling apart. A country that spends billions to fund its arsenal of nuclear weapons, forces its poor to eat grass. The suicide rate among the poor, driven insane by poverty, has risen sharply over the last decade. In January 1998, a transport worker in Hyderabad, who had not been paid for two years, soaked himself in petrol and set himself alight outside the Press Club. He left behind a letter:

'I have lost patience. Me and my fellow-workers have been

*Nawaz Sharif and his family helped create a culture in which they genuinely believed that everything was for sale, including politicians, civil servants and, yes, generals.*

protesting the non-payment of our salaries for a long time. But nobody takes any notice. My wife and mother are seriously ill and I have no money for their treatment. My family is starving and I am fed up with quarrels. I don't have the right to live. I am sure the flames of my body will reach the houses of the rich one day.'

Nawaz Sharif, his brother, Shahbaz and their father, Muhammed, strong believers in globalisation and neo-liberal economics, helped create an enterprise culture in which they genuinely believed that everything was for sale, including politicians, civil servants and, yes, generals. There were widespread rumours that, in order to buy time and make yet more money, the Sharif family had provided sackfuls of general-friendly dollars to bolster their support in the army. A section of the army high command was enraged by this civilian interference.

The immediate cause of the latest coup was Sharif's decision to sack the army chief, General Musharraf, while he was on an official visit to Sri Lanka, and appoint the head of Inter Services Intelligence (ISI), General Ziauddin, in his place. Just as Pakistan TV was showing Sharif appointing and congratulating the new army chief, the old army pulled the plug and the country's TV screens went blank. Ziauddin, as the ISI boss, was the main supplier of the Taliban army in Afghanistan. He was sympathetic to the fundamentalist cause and loathed by officers who value the secular side of the army and enjoy drinking whisky to the tune of bagpipes at regimental dinners. Musharraf's supporters inside the army moved swiftly. Once Nawaz Sharif's instruction that the plane returning the general

*The bloated Pakistani Army hated becoming a Cold War orphan, and threw a nuclear tantrum.*

to Pakistan be diverted to a foreign country was ignored and Musharraf landed at a Karachi airport secured by the army, it became obvious that the government would be toppled.

The bloated Pakistan army — one of the Pentagon's spoilt brats in Asia — hated becoming a Cold War orphan. 'Pakistan was the condom the Americans needed to enter Afghanistan,' a retired general told me in 1998. 'We've served our purpose and they think we can just be flushed down the toilet.' In 1998, the army, fearful that a forced rapprochement with India might lead to a relegation of its status and power and a reduction of its budget, played the nuclear card. This was followed by an adventurous border with India in Kargil during which Pakistan received a severe drubbing. This increased tensions with the government which tried to pin the entire blame for the botched operation on the army. Now Musharraf has seized power in the country, but in changed conditions.

Several months prior to the 12 October 1999 coup, I had visited Lahore. Islamabad remains the official capital, but real power, before the coup, was exercised from the Punjabi capital of Lahore. When I visited, it was glistening in the spring sun. This city, dry, warm and abundant, where I spent the first twenty years of my life and which I still love, is forever changing, usually for the worse.

The old Mall at its lower end, near Kim's Gun, was once the haunt of bohemians of every type. Poets, artists, leftist intellectuals, film directors could be seen at their tables in the Coffee House, cursing the military dictator of the day or discussing the merits of blank verse as they dipped their samosas in a mint-chilly compote and sipped tea throughout the month of

Ramadan. That was over thirty years ago. Queen Victoria's statue which once graced the city in front of the Punjab assembly building, has long since gone. Some imaginative soul decided to replace history with fantasy. A giant stone Koran is poised precariously on the plinth where the Queen once sat.

There are still pockets of dissent and resistance and idealism. There has been a long line of tormented solitary figures bemoaning the fate of the nation, but greed and self-interest and despair are stamped on too many faces now.

The Mall, Lahore's principal thoroughfare, linking the Civil Lines and cantonment of the old colonial city to the old bazaars and monuments of the Mughal Empire, is choked with pollution caused by the exhaust-pipes of an unending stream of cars and taxis which cannot travel at more than five miles an hour. It is noticeable that a much-favoured taxi and rickshaw pin-up these days is Osama Bin Laden. The US state department's 'most wanted terrorist' is well on his way to becoming a Pakistani hero. Nor is his popularity confined to the plebeian sections of the city. Many middle-class students are searching for extreme solutions via their religion.

One can get to know the whole country more through Lahore than any other city because Pakistan, since the defection of Bangladesh, is really an extended Punjab. The provinces of Sindh, Balochistan and the Frontier are sparsely populated and largely tribal and rural. The latest excitement in Lahore was the opening of PACE, a large supermarket (whose owners included Imran Khan) in the heart of Gulberg, which was once a salubrious and spacious residential area, but has now succumbed to the lure of small and big businesses.

The entrance to PACE attracted more visitors than the actual goods on display. Peasants with marvellous moustaches,

*Lahore in the epoch of globalisation — the PACE supermarket.*

anointed with mustard seed oil, came from nearby villages with their entire families. They packed the foyer and both adults and children, half-fearful, half-excited, screamed with pleasure as they travelled up and down on the new escalators. It could have been a scene from nineteenth century Paris, but it wasn't. This was Lahore in the epoch of globalisation. A Lahore where the intrusive noise caused by competing loudspeakers in neighbouring mosques compels one to cease work or conversation and plug one's ears.

Not far from PACE, hidden away in a tiny lane, is one of the new architectural glories of Lahore: the newly-constructed Institute for Women's Studies, a residential post-graduate college for South Asian women. The very idea of such a centre has enraged the beards. But the director of the institute, Nighat 'Bunny' Khan, remains unperturbed. Struck by the remarkable quality of the building being shown to me, I wonder aloud as to which of the country's top architects were involved.

'None of them', replies Bunny, her gruff voice tinged with pride. 'We decided to commission a woman, Fawzia Qureshi. She's a senior lecturer in architecture at the National College of Art. This was her first big commission.'

Qureshi has used a tiny plot of land to build a structure on three levels in which the use of light and space is exemplary. The essential purpose of the building, which gives it its special character, is sociability and a sense of community. The building, with its courtyard and terraces and seminar rooms bathed throughout the day in natural light, is a carefully arranged marriage of modernism and native Islamic tradition. But how long will Bunny's creation last? She remains a determined and dedicated feminist, in a land where rural women are still shackled to men.

In the remoter districts of Sindh and tribal Balochistan, women are still being killed for bringing 'dishonour' to their families. This usually means that a woman who refuses to marry a man chosen by her father or has an extra-marital affair is despatched without ceremony. The writ of the Pakistani state does not extend to these regions. Everyone knows the identity of the killers but the police remain aloof. It is a matter for the family and the village elders.

Feminist lawyers and human rights activists have tried for many decades to turn the tide and with some success. This was one area where the Benazir government was genuinely more enlightened. But the same delicate hand of Benazir that signed a decree setting up more facilities for women also authorised the arming of the Taliban and the assault on Kabul. The Nawaz Sharif government, for its part, was pushing through religious laws designed to make women second-class citizens. And hacks in the employ of his government had already begun to denounce Bunny and her institute as a nest of atheists and communists. The usual tag in these circumstances is 'lesbian' but the word does not exist in the Urdu or Punjabi vocabulary, something of which I had been unaware till then. No such inhibitions mar the colourful phrases used to describe male homosexuality, incest and bestiality.

W hen I was in Pakistan earlier, in 1996, the surface calm was deceptive. As I was lunching with my mother in her favourite Islamabad restaurant, a jovial moustachioed figure came over to greet us from an adjacent table. His wife, Benazir, was abroad on a state visit. He was responsible for entertaining the children and had brought them out for a special treat. An exchange of pleasantries ensued. I asked how things were proceeding in the country. 'Fine,' he replied with a charming grin. 'All is well.' He should have known better.

Behind closed doors in the capital, Islamabad, a palace coup was in motion. Benazir was about to be luxuriously betrayed. Her hand-picked president, Farooq Leghari, after secret consultations with the army and leaders of Opposition, was preparing to dismiss her government. During dinner that same week, an old acquaintance, now a senior civil servant and very fond of Benazir, was in a state of despair. He described how the president had sought to defuse the crisis by asking for a special meeting with the prime minister. Benazir, characteristically, turned up with her husband, Senator Asif Zardari, the state minister for investment. This annoyed Leghari, since one of the subjects he had wished to discuss with her was her husband's legendary rapaciousness and greed.

Despite the irritation, he remained serene while attempting to convince the First Couple that it was not simply their traditional political enemies or smaller-sized brains who were demanding action. The scale of the corruption and the corresponding decay of the administration had become a national scandal. As president of the country, he was under pressure from the army and concerned groups of citizens to act against her government. In order to resist them, he needed her help. He pleaded with her to discipline her husband and other out-of-control ministers. At this point Zardari, stubbornly consistent in defending his own material interests, grinned and taunted the president with the remark that nobody in Pakistan, including Leghari, had a clean slate. The threat was obvious. You touch us and we'll expose you.

Leghari felt that the dignity of his office had been insulted. He began to tremble with anger. He suggested that Zardari leave the room. Benazir nodded and Zardari walked out. Alone now with his prime minister, except for the discreet presence of a civil servant, he once again entreated her to restrain her turbulent husband. She smiled patronisingly and gave her president a little lecture on how much she valued loyalty. The people who were complaining, she told him, were jealous of her husband's business acumen. They were professional whiners, has-beens, rogues resentful at being bypassed when top jobs were being allocated. She made no concessions.

By Pakistani standards Leghari is an honest, straightforward man. He was Benazir's choice as president only because

*Benazir thought Leghari would be a loyal president but he sacked her when she refused to restrain her husband Asif Zardari and other corrupt ministers.*

she thought he lacked ambition and would do her will. He would be a good dog. Disappointed aspirants were told: 'He may not be very bright. He's a bit limited, but his heart is in the right place.'

**13**

Last year, Leghari told me that this meeting, the last of many, had been decisive. His patience had evaporated. He could no longer tolerate her excesses. He believed that if she continued in office the army would intervene and murder democracy for the fourth time in the country's chequered history. Reluctantly, he decided to utilise the hated Eighth Amendment (a gift to the nation from the late General Zia, which gave the president powers to dismiss an elected government) and dismissed the government. New elections were to be held within ninety days.

Immediately after Benazir's fall, Zardari was arrested. To this day he languishes in a Karachi prison, charged with a series of offences for which government lawyers have yet to find proof acceptable in a Pakistani court, where standards of evidence are exceptionally low. The state has yet to find a reliable witness. Zardari's business associates and friends have remained loyal. One of them, the chairman of Pakistan Steel, chose to commit suicide rather than bear witness against his former patron. Some of Benazir's closest supporters — and they exist — are insistent that her political prestige was squandered by a husband who is a fraud, a poseur, a wastrel, a philanderer and much worse.

A few years ago, while addressing a friendly gathering at a seminar in Islamabad, Benazir attempted to defend the quondam minister for investment. He was much misunderstood, she said, but before she could continue the members of the audience began to shake their heads in disapproval and shout 'No! No! No!' She paused and then said with a sigh: 'I wonder why I always get the same reaction whenever I mention him?' Either the question was tongue-in-cheek or lust is truly blind.

I don't think Zardari was the only reason for her unpopularity. Unfortunately, her People's Party government did little for the poor of town and country that constitute its natural constituency. Most of her ministers at the national and provincial levels were so busy lining their own pockets that they failed to notice how the lining of the stomachs of poverty-stricken children was being affected by the shortage of food and the lack of a proper diet. Infant mortality figures remained unchanged throughout her period in office.

Benazir, permanently encircled by cronies and sycophants, had become isolated from her electorate and oblivious to reality. In the general election following her removal from power, her People's Party suffered a humiliating defeat. The Pakistani electorate may be largely illiterate, but its political sophistication has never been in doubt. The mood was one of disillusionment. Disappointment had created apathy and weariness. Benazir's supporters refused to vote for her, but they could not bring themselves to vote for the enemy. Instead, they stayed at home. The Muslim League won its giant majority (over two-third of the seats in the national assembly) on the basis of a minority vote. Only twenty-five per cent of those eligible bothered to visit the polling-booths.

Since 1947, Lahore has been the home-town of the ruling Sharif family. They were blacksmiths in East Punjab (now in India) and sought refuge in the new Muslim homeland. They worked hard. Their foundries prospered. They were disinterested in politics. One day, in 1972, Benazir's father,

Zulfiqar Ali Bhutto, was advised to nationalise the Sharif family factory. It was an economically inept decision, but it pleased party loyalists and it distracted attention from the fact that Bhutto had failed to push through badly-needed land reforms in the countryside. The landlords were only too pleased to support the half-baked nationalisation of industries large and small. One of the results of all this was to make Muhammed Sharif, the family patriarch, a lifelong enemy of Bhutto. When General Zia took over in July 1977, the Sharif clan cheered loudly. When Zia ordered the execution of Bhutto after a rigged trial, the Sharif family gave thanks to Allah for answering their prayers. The continuing rivalry between Bhutto's daughter, Benazir, and Muhammed's son, Nawaz, has rich antecedents.

Nawaz Sharif became Zia's protégé and was brought into politics as the clumsy, dirty boot of the ISI, the most powerful institution in the country. In his last government, Sharif's

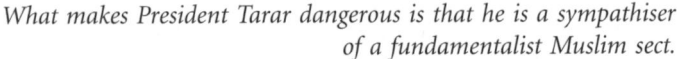

*What makes President Tarar dangerous is that he is a sympathiser of a fundamentalist Muslim sect.*

brother, Shahbaz, was the chief minister of Punjab and their Abbaji ('dear father'), Muhammed, was amusing himself in his dotage by sponsoring the appointment of old cronies as ambassadors and even selected the president of the country. The current incumbent, a bearded simpleton called Rafiq Tarar, is one of Abbaji's factotums. What makes Tarar dangerous is that he is a sympathiser of the fundamentalist Muslim sect of the Deobandi Tablighis.

Of the two brothers, Shahbaz is perceived as a more sophisticated politician. Post-Kargil, the US embassy had organised his trip to Washington for a meeting with Sandy Berger at the White House. It is now an open secret that Washington would have liked to swap the brothers by sending Shahbaz to the Prime Minister's House and giving Nawaz his old job — the chief ministership of Punjab — in Lahore.

Nothing changed during the rule of the Sharif brothers, but then few expected anything to happen. Corruption, its tentacles spreading from the top downwards, was so widespread that visiting economists from the World Bank and the International Monetary Fund (IMF) were, like Kurtz in Conrad's *Heart of Darkness*, traumatised by the scale of the horror. Local wits express bewilderment at the news that Nigeria heads the list of the world's most corrupt countries. 'Even here,' they say as they shed mock tears, 'we can't quite make the top. Why didn't we bribe the agency compiling the statistics?'

The elite, led by the politicians, continued to loot the country's wealth. Benazir's gang had had its turn and it was back to the Sharif brothers. Less than one per cent of Pakistan's population pays income tax. The politicians, many of whom are landlords, refuse to countenance a serious agricultural tax. State-owned banks have been shamelessly pillaged. Forced by successive governments to loan money to politicians, landlords and businessmen, the banks are not encouraged to retrieve the money. Bad bank loans stand at two hundred billion rupees, which is the rough equivalent of seventy per cent of the total revenue base of the country's budget. Pakistan marks the new millennium with a foreign debt of forty-two billion dollars and a domestic debt of seventy billion dollars, a combined figure that is fifty billion dollars higher than the Gross Domestic Product of the country.

While I was there in 1999, the army had been asked by the government to take over the Water and Power Development Authority (WAPDA) and ensure that all electricity bills were paid on time. Soldiers arrived at every house to read the electricity meters and discovered ingenious methods being utilised to slow down the meter or to steal electricity directly from the supply system by circumventing the WAPDA wires. Interestingly, most of these schemes involved those who could afford to pay their bills, including a wealthy landowner who was a minister in the Sharif government. Despite the evidence, she continued to plead innocent, refused to resign and ultimately, because of a media campaign, was sacked from her post.

Though the army is in charge now, past experience has shown that officers and soldiers soon get infected by the cancer of corruption. A recent joke in Lahore was based on the rumour that Nawaz Sharif, on Abbaji's advice, had kept the army at bay by bribing corps commanders with money-bags containing one crore rupees for each general. A wit suggested that the title should be changed from corps commanders to crore commanders. Sections of the army high command, including Musharraf, were livid at this attempt to destroy the unity of the officer corps. Attempts to appease him failed and a plot was hatched to remove him as chief of staff. The result is now history. Everything backfired, triggering off a new period of military rule. The state had once again come full circle.

Underneath all this chicanery the country continues to rot. A state that has never provided free education or health can now no longer guarantee subsidised wheat, rice or sugar and nor can it protect innocent lives from random killings. The country's largest city, Karachi, has been in a state of virtual civil war for an entire decade. On one side are the Urdu-speaking children of the refugees who trekked to the new homeland from India in 1947. Their organisation, the MQM (Mohajir Qaumi Mahaz — National Organisation of Refugees) has waged war on indigenous Sindhis as well as the government. Several thousand on both sides have died in armed encounters.

It is this abdication of its traditional role by a corrupt and decaying state combined with the surreal neo-liberal economic prescriptions handed down by the politburos of the IMF and World Bank that has created the space for political Islam.

In successive general elections, the people have voted against hardline religious parties. The Pakistan electorate, for instance, casts proportionately fewer votes for religious fundamentalists than voters in Israel. The strength of religious extremism, till now, has come from state patronage rather than popular support. The groups that are currently paralysing the country were the creation of Zia, who received political, military and financial support from the US and Britain throughout his eleven years as dictator of Pakistan. The West needed Zia to fight their Afghan war against the former Soviet Union. Nothing else mattered. The CIA turned a blind eye to the sale of heroin supposedly to fund the Afghan war. The number of officially registered heroin addicts in Pakistan rose from 130 in 1977 to 30,000 in 1988.

*It was during Zia's regime (1977-88) that a network of madrassas was established with a clear aim: to produce fanatics.*

It was during this period (1977-88) that a network of madrassas (religious boarding schools) was established throughout the country. Initially, most of these were funded by foreign aid from a variety of sources. These schools became the training ground for a new religious 'scholar'. Since boarding and lodging were free, it was not only the children of poor Afghan refugees who flocked to receive this privileged and unique instruction. Poor peasant families were only too happy to donate a son to the madrassas. They thought it would be a mouth less to feed at home and the boy would be educated and might find a job in the city or, if he was really lucky, in one of the Gulf states.

Together with verses from the Koran (to be learnt by rote) and the necessity to lead a devout life, these children were taught to banish all doubts. The only truth was divine truth and the only code of conduct was that written in the Koran and the hadiths. Virtue lay in unthinking obedience. Anyone who rebels against the imam rebels against Allah. The aim was clear. These madrassas had a single function. They were nurseries designed to produce fanatics. The primers, for example, stated that the Urdu letter jeem stood for jihad; tay for tope (cannon); kaaf for Kalashnikov and khay for khoon (blood).

As they grew older they were instructed in the use of sophisticated hand weapons and taught how to make and plant bombs. ISI agents provided training and supervision. They could also observe the development of the more promising students or the Taliban, who were later picked out and sent for more specialised training at secret army camps, the better to fight the 'holy war' against the unbelievers in Afghanistan.

Pakistan's oldest Islamic party, the Jamaat-i-Islami, had grown in influence during the Zia years. Its leaders assumed that they would run the schools. The party has always prided itself on its cadre organisation built on the underground 'Leninist model' of small cells. It shunned mass membership, but this may have been because it, in turn, was shunned by the masses. Its leaders now thought their time had come. They saw the students as potential recruits. They were to be disappointed. New problems arose. Since dollars were freely available, different Islamic factions emerged and began to compete with each other for mastery in these schools and a division of the spoils. The ISI became the arbiter of intra-religious disputes and favoured some groups against others.

For a time the Afghan war consumed their energies. After the first war was over, the Pakistani state refused to accept a coalition government in Afghanistan. It was Benazir Bhutto's government that unleashed the Taliban, backed by Pakistan army commando units, in an attempt to take Kabul. The US, fearful of Iranian influence in the region, had backed this decision.

The dragon seeds sown in 2,500 madrassas produced a crop of 225,000 fanatics ready to kill and die for their faith when ordered to do so by their religious leaders. Gen. Naseerullah Babar, Benazir's minister for the interior, confided to friends that since the Taliban were becoming a menace inside Pakistan, he had decided that the only solution to the problem lay in giving the extremists their own country. This argument was disingenuous at the time, but in the light of what has happened over the last two years, Babar deserves to be tried as a war-criminal.

With the collapse of the Soviet Union, the Cold War came to an end, leaving behind orphan-states on every continent. The effect in Pakistan was catastrophic. The fundamentalist groups had served their purpose and, unsurprisingly, the US no longer felt the need to supply them with funds and weaponry. Overnight, the latter became violently anti-American and began to dream of revenge. Pakistan's political and military leaders, who had served the US loyally and continuously from 1951 onwards, felt humiliated by Washington's indifference.

The Pakistani Army refused to be relegated to the status of Kuwait. In order to gain attention it threw a nuclear tantrum. The explosion has had the desired effect. Pakistan is back on the 'B list' of countries in the US state department. On 29 November 1998, the then foreign minister, Sartaj Aziz, attempted to soothe Western opinion: 'I see no possibility of an accidental nuclear war between Pakistan and India. Pakistan has an effective control and command system.' This is pure nonsense on a scientific level, but even if one were to accept the statement, a political question is immediately posed. What if reality began to imitate our nightmares and the Taliban took over the Pakistani Army? Every political leader in Pakistan is aware of the danger. Nawaz Sharif attempted to pre-empt political Islam by stealing some of its clothes, but this is a tactic that rarely works and is usually a mark of desperation.

The irony of the present situation is that religion in the Punjab was always a relaxed affair. The old tradition of Sufi mysticism, with its emphasis on individual communion with the Creator and its hostility to preachers, had found deep roots in the countryside. The tombs of the old Sufi saints, for centuries the site of annual festivals during which the participants sang, danced, drank, inhaled bhang and fornicated to their heart's content, were placed under martial law by Zia. The people were to be denied simple pleasures.

The arrival of a peculiarly non-Punjabi form of religious extremism did not arrive in Pakistan from nowhere. It was approved by Washington, funded by Saudi petrodollars and carefully nourished by Zia. The result was the birth of madness. The twisted and self-destructive character of the

*Every religious faction in Pakistan now lays claim to Islam and disputes are no longer settled through discussions, but resolved by machine-guns and massacres.*

groups that have been mushrooming over the last five years is hardly in doubt. Ninety per cent of Pakistan's Muslims are Sunnis. The rest are mainly Shias. The Sunnis themselves are divided into two major schools of thought. The Deobandis represent orthodoxy. The Barelvis believe in a more synthetic Islam, defined and changed by local conditions. For many years these were literary disputes, often debated in public by mullahs and religious scholars. No longer. Every faction now lays claim to Islam, a moral and political claim. Disputes are no longer settled through discussion, but resolved by machine-guns and massacres.

Some Deobandi factions want the Shias to be declared as heretics and, preferably, physically exterminated. A sectarian civil war has been raging for nearly three years. The Sunni Sipah-e-Sahaba (Soldiers of the First Four Caliphs) has attacked Shia mosques in the heart of Lahore and massacred the Shia faithful at prayer. The Shias have responded in kind. They formed the Sipah-e-Mohammed (Soldiers of Mohammed), got Iranian backing and began to exact a gruesome revenge. Several hundred people have died in these intra-Muslim massacres, mainly Shias.

In January this year, an armed Taliban faction seized a whole group of villages in the Hangu district of Pakistan's North West Frontier Province. They declared the area to be under 'Islamic laws' and promptly proceeded to organise the public destruction of TV sets and dish antennae in the village of Zargari. This was followed by the burning of 3000 'obscene' video and audio cassettes in the small square in Lukki.

There is something slightly comical in this hostility to television and it reminds one of a situationist spectacle in the 1960s, but humour, alas, is not something associated with the

Taliban. The leader of the movement, Hussain Jalali, wants to extend the Afghan experience to Pakistan. After the television burning, he declared: 'The hands and feet of thieves will be chopped off and all criminals brought to justice in accordance with Islamic laws.'

'What can we do?' a supporter of the Sharif brothers had asked me, wringing his hands in despair. 'These bastards are all armed!' I pointed out that some of the bastards were being armed by the government to create mayhem in neighbouring Kashmir, but that Pakistan's bloated army was also armed. Why weren't they asked to disarm these groups? Here the conversation ended. For it is no secret that the fundamentalists have penetrated the army on every level. What distinguishes them from the old-style religious groups is that they want to seize state power and for that they need the army.

*What distinguishes the new extreme religious groups from the old is that they now want to seize state power. For that they need the army which they have penetrated at every level.*

*The Lashkar-e-Toeba militants are trained by the army at eight camps in 'Azaad' Kashmir and funded by Saudi Arabia and the Pakistan government.*

In fact, one of the most virulent of the groups, the Lashkar-e-Toeba (Soldiers of Medina), is a creation of the ISI. Its political wing, Ahle Hadis, wants the Saudi model implanted in Pakistan, but without the monarchy. They have supporters and mosques throughout the world, including Britain and the US, whose aim is to supply cadres and money for the worldwide jehad. The Ahle Hadis is the most orthodox of the Sunni sects and is in a minority except that it has powerful supporters — government ministers grace its meetings. Their sub-office is at 5 Chamberlaine Road in Lahore. I was tempted to go and interview them, but the sight of thirty heavily-armed guards decided me against the venture.

The group's armed wing, the Lashkar-e-Toeba, could not exist without the patronage of the army. It has a membership of fifty thousand militants and is the leading group in the jehad to 'liberate' Indian Kashmir. They are trained by the army at eight special camps in 'Azaad' (Pakistani-controlled) Kashmir and are funded by Saudi Arabia and the government of Pakistan. They recruit teenagers from poor families for the holy war. They have lost several hundred members in Kashmir. The government pays them fifty thousand rupees for each corpse returned from Kashmir. While fifteeen thousand rupees are paid to the family of the 'martyr', the rest helps to fund the organisation.

The Harkat ul-Ansar (Volunteers Movement), once funded by the US and backed by the ISI, was declared a terrorist organisation by the state department last year. It promptly changed its name to Harkat ul-Mujahideen. Its fighters were amongst the most dedicated Taliban and it has shifted its training camps from the Punjab to Afghanistan. The Saudi terrorist, Osama Bin Laden, continues to maintain close contacts with the ISI and his supporters have warned the government that any attempt to abduct him or ban his organisation would lead to an immediate civil war in Pakistan. They boast that the army will never agree to be used against them. Why? Because there has been a symbiosis of sorts. There are too many of their supporters in the army and on every level.

Both these groups want to take over Pakistan. They dream of an Islamic Federation which will impose a Pax Talibana stretching from Lahore to Samarkand, but avoiding the 'Heretics Republic of Iran'. For all their incoherence and senseless rage, their message is attractive to those layers of the population who yearn for some order in their lives. If the fanatics promise to feed them and educate their children, they are prepared to forego the delights of CNN and BBC World. It is this that is truly frightening.

The only other alternative is to mend the breach with India. The 1998 visit of the Indian prime minister, Atal Behari Vajpayee, to Lahore was welcomed by business interests and an otherwise critical print media. There is a great deal of talk of a new permanent settlement. An EU-style arrangement that incorporates India, Pakistan, Bangladesh and Sri Lanka. An opening of the frontiers and a no-war pact between India and Pakistan. It is undoubtedly the most rational solution on offer, but it would necessitate the disarming of, at least, the Lashkar-e-Toeba. During his visit, the Indian prime minister had demanded this as a gesture of goodwill.

When a leader of the group was informed of this request by a Pakistani official, he replied: 'Try and disarm us, if you can. If you do we will have to do now what we were planning to do in two years' time. It's up to you.' It is this desire for a head-on clash, this urge towards an explosive encounter, even if they turn out to be the victims of such an encounter, that marks the new wave of Islamic militants in Pakistan. Mercifully, they still constitute a minority in the country, but all that could change if nothing else changes.

Has anything really changed with the coup of 12 October 1999? Most of the liberal intelligentsia, disillusioned with traditional political alternatives and too exhausted to act themselves, were hopeful that Musharraf would modernise the structure, but the underlying problems refuse to go away. Good intentions alone cannot change Pakistan. The problem posed by the existence of armed fundamentalist organisations cannot be solved by adopting an ostrich pose.

The army is no longer a unified institution. Well-organised groups of Islamic zealots have penetrated its core. Unlike the older and more traditional religious parties, the Sipah-e-Sahaba, the Sipah-e-Mohammed, the Lashkar-e-Toeba and the Harkat ul-Mujahideen are all hungry for power. Their preferred model is that of the Taliban. If such a faction were ever to take over the Pakistani Army — and the possibility is not as remote as it seemed a few years ago — the possession of nuclear weapons would acquire a frightening new significance.

That, too, will achieve little, for the only serious and rational alternative to domestic chaos is a long-term Treaty of Friendship and Trade with India, a new permanent settlement which could form the basis of a larger EU-style confederation of South Asian Republics. Within such a framework the Kashmir question, too, could be amicably resolved. After all, it should be perfectly possible for both India and Pakistan to guarantee an autonomous Kashmir within such a confederation. In fact, Kashmir could become a haven of peace, symbolising a new peaceful coexistence. If the political will existed in Delhi and the GHQ in Rawalpindi what I am suggesting is perfectly achievable.

For over fifty years, Pakistan has turned its back on India, imagining it could replace its giant neighbour by cultivating links with the Gulf states and Saudi Arabia. (The only exception was in 1961 when Ayub Khan, under US influence, offered a joint defence pact to India. Nehru retorted: 'Joint defence against whom?' The answer came a year later on the Sino-Indian border. Interestingly enough, the joint defence proposal aroused very little protest in Pakistan itself!) The strategy has been a political and economic failure, leaving the country denuded of a skilled labour-force and incapable of meeting its own basic needs. In recent years, there were a few signs that politicians of the main secular parties were beginning to explore a new economic deal with India. Pressure from the fundamentalists and the army sent their heads quickly back into the sand. And yet this remains the only rational solution in the medium term. All other options are bleak beyond belief.

The ISI-armed fundamentalists are waiting in the wings. The hijacking of an Indian Airlines plane and the release of a fundamentalist leader was merely a symptom of the dangers that lurk underneath the surface of Pakistan's social fabric. Previous civilian governments could not guarantee law and order outside a few cities. If the army too fails in this respect the future could be unpredictable and chaotic. If they decide to split the army it would unleash a bloody civil war, with devastating consequences for the entire region. If the politicians of the subcontinent fail to devise a way of living together, they might end up dying together. India, as the largest and most powerful of South Asian states, needs to take a serious peace initiative in the region and to make offers to its neighbours which are difficult to reject.

# The Last, Losing Bet

## S. AKBAR ZAIDI

The former professor of economics at the University of Karachi on how the civil society in Pakistan is wrong in welcoming General Musharraf, and why he is bound to fail.

The events of 12 October 1999 have only confirmed the view that it is the military which has always held supreme power and ruled Pakistan, despite a period of democracy which lasted almost eleven years. None of the four elected governments in this period — two of Benazir Bhutto and two of Nawaz Sharif — completed its tenure. While three of these governments were dismissed by the president, who had the constitutional right and provision to do so under the Eighth Amendment of the Constitution of Pakistan, this time round the president no longer had the power and the military has acted unconstitutionally.

Gen. Pervez Musharraf, in his second address to the nation, said that rather than let the entire body (of Pakistan) rot and break away by following the Constitution, he decided to amputate a leg (the Constitution) and save the rest of the body. He has put the Constitution in abeyance until he and the military decide that it is time to hold elections again and to resume the process of democracy under far different conditions and rules. (Now where have we heard all this before?) While martial law has not as yet been declared, and the so-called chief executive has spoken about not interfering with basic freedoms, including that of the press, the national and provincial assemblies have been suspended, though not dismissed. Numerous elected and appointed government functionaries are being held without any cases against them, while many others, including ambassadors, have been arbitrarily removed from their previous posts and assignments, without any explanation and reason given for this action by the military. So much for this brand of accountability.

The chief executive's immediate agenda includes the aim to rebuild national confidence and morale, strengthen the federation, revive the economy, provide better governance, decentralisation and devolution, speedy law and justice and, of course, the accountability of those who have held power in the past. Importantly, none of the orders of the chief executive can be challenged by any court or law in the country.

The military coup has been unanimously well received in Pakistan. All political parties, including important members of the dismissed Muslim League, and all the combined opposition, have welcomed Musharraf's intrusion. Even those so-called liberals and champions of democracy who fought against General Zia's military dictatorship are now writing articles justifying his takeover, arguing that this is the only way Pakistan can be saved from certain catastrophe. Citing the example of East Asia, they argue that authoritarian rule provides effective results. They say that Nawaz Sharif would have led this country

*The elite in Pakistan support Musharraf because they want instant solutions, irrespective of how they are to be achieved.*

towards destruction within a matter of a few years; by gambling on the military, they are hoping that this will not happen. And if it does, some say, well, it was always inevitable. The military, they argue, is their last bet.

What the reaction of the so-called liberal and pro-democracy elements in Pakistan towards Musharraf reveals is that this important section does not consider democracy to be a process which takes time, often generations, but rather, a mechanism which puts in place instant solutions irrespective of how they are to be achieved. While they talk about 'institutions' and institution-building, they are not concerned with how these interventions take place, or who builds institutions in their own preferred manner. Most importantly, the process of building democratic institutions in a country which has had military rule for almost half of its fifty-two years, is not considered important enough.

Call it opportunism or a lack of hope, or one last bet, but the public in Pakistan has overlooked a number of important facts that have taken place in recent times. All the attacks against Nawaz Sharif since his ouster have centred around the fact that his was a one-man autocratic government. Yet, while people welcome Musharraf as their saviour, they conveniently ignore the fact that military rule is always a one-man rule and potentially far worse than any form of autocratic democracy. Besides, while democracy does always have the military as a potential watchdog if things get out of hand, history has shown that the military, once entrenched in power, does not leave easily. The previous two military dictators in Pakistan, Gen. Ayub Khan and Gen. Zia ul-Haq, did not leave of their free will. It took extraordinary events to remove both — Ayub went only after mass protest against his rule in 1969, two years before the creation of Bangladesh and Zia was killed in a plane crash believed to have been administered by the army itself. It is improbable, therefore, that Musharraf will go on his own. In fact, the worst-case scenario would be: Musharraf fails to revive the economy and there is a counter-coup from within the military led by an Islamist Talibanesque-type of general.

*It is being overlooked that the orders of the chief executive cannot be challenged by any court in Pakistan. Who will hold the army accountable?*

Secondly, while our good liberal friends endorse the measures taken by Musharraf to initiate the process of accountability of Nawaz Sharif and his cronies, they conveniently overlook the fact that the orders of the chief executive cannot be challenged by any court in Pakistan. Moreover, his dismissal of the government itself and the abeyance of the Constitution are both illegal. Who will hold the army accountable?

Thirdly, all the ground that had been covered by the liberal lobby after the Pakistan army's fiasco in Kargil, in terms of discussing the role of the military in Pakistan's economy, has certainly been lost. After Kargil, many of us questioned the amount budgeted for the military each year, and there was a possibility that the voices of democracy may have put some

*After Kargil, there was some pressure on the military to reveal its accounts; after the coup that opportunity has been lost for good.*

pressure on the military to reveal its accounts. Clearly, that opportunity has been lost for good. (Defence expenditure is around five per cent of the GDP; each year, fifty-one per cent of Pakistan's budget goes to debt servicing, i.e. interest payments on previous loans, and about twenty-eight per cent to the military.) Linked to the issue of the military revealing its accounts was the possibility of peace in South Asia, with the

BJP (Bharatiya Janata Party) and Nawaz governments talking peace and moving towards economic and trade relations to start with. This too, has been put aside for the moment.

There has always been a great sense of relief, if not out-right euphoria, whenever a government is dismissed in Pakistan, particularly since the dismissal of the first Benazir government in 1990. However, the difference this time round is that the military itself has assumed complete power, and despite its attempt to construct a civilian charade, few would contest the claim that Pakistan is more or less under martial law. This is probably the main reason why expectations this time are higher; the assumption is that unlike the politicians in the past, the military may actually deliver on its promises. This belief rests on the premise that in the context of Pakistan, it is military rule which is actually 'good for the people' and delivers basic development services and goods. The years of martial law under Ayub and Zia are supposed to bear testimony to this claim. In contrast, democracy is seen to be a rule of greed, avarice and corruption, where the only bene-ficiaries are politicians in power and their cronies.

The dichotomy between democracy and dictatorship in terms of what they mean for development is perhaps the best and most simplistic of myths accepted by the general public, scholars and policy-makers. Most people in Pakistan recall Ayub Khan's rule (1958-69) as Pakistan's 'best,' with Zia's (1977-88) a close second. In contrast, the democratic years of Zulfiqar Ali Bhutto, his daughter Benazir or of Nawaz Sharif, reveal only the worst manifestations of democracy. Yet, these 'facts' reveal only half the true picture.

*Ayub's decade was impressive mainly because of the economic
exploitation of East Pakistan (now Bangladesh).*

Ayub Khan's decade of development was indeed that, a
period of exemplary growth for the economy. In the 1960s,
Pakistan's economy grew by 6.8 per cent a year, no mean
achievement for a country that began with very little. Agricultural growth rates were on average 5.1 per cent per annum
in the decade, and the industrial sector showed even more
impressive rates, of 9.9 per cent growth per annum. Zia's eleven
years (1977-88) were equally impressive, with the economy
growing by about 6.5 per cent annually, agriculture by 5.4 per
cent, and industry by 8.2 per cent. Moreover, for the period
1980-88, Pakistan's GDP growth rate was recognised by the
World Bank as the fourth highest in the world. In contrast, in
the five-and-a-half years under Zulfiqar Ali Bhutto, the economy
grew on average by 4.4 per cent per annum, with agriculture

and industry growing by a mere two per cent on average, each; inflation too, in this period, averaged fourteen per cent. Worse still has been the performance of the economy in the post-1988 democracy period, easily labelled as the worst decade in Pakistan's history. Ergo, military dictatorship is far better than democracy.

It is indeed unfortunate that most people reach that conclusion from the facts above, for they ignore far too many features of Pakistan's society, economics and politics that have been the cause of these statistics. Moreover, numerous consequences of these high achievements are also ignored.

Ayub Khan's decade was truly impressive, although much of the explanation for the growth under him is to be found in the economic and political exploitation of East Pakistan (now Bangladesh), as resources were transferred from the eastern wing of the country to the western part. Without the ample use of foreign exchange earned from jute, which was later invested in West Pakistan, it is improbable that these high rates of growth (in West Pakistan) would have taken place. The end result of this Golden Age in Pakistan was the secession of the majority province (East Pakistan) after a brutal and ignoble war which West Pakistan lost.

The two main factors behind Zia's achievements are easier to explain: remittances worth twenty-three billion dollars sent back over ten years by Pakistani workers in the Gulf states which helped fuel the services and industrial sectors; and military and economic aid in huge quantities from the Western world, following the Russian invasion of Afghanistan. While there was impressive economic growth, the downside was reflected in unprecedented schisms in society, with ethnic and sectarian violence raging in numerous parts of the country; the coming

*While Bhutto's bad performance had more to do with bad luck,*
*Pakistan is still haunted by the demons Zia unleashed.*

in of a culture now known as the Kalashnikov and heroin
culture; a parallel black economy which began to undermine
the real economy; raging budget deficits; active discrimination
and sanctified violence against minorities and women; and a
host of other factors which have continued to haunt Pakistan

to this day. Zia was not concerned with society or its development and merely wanted to consolidate power. The negative impact of his rule left Pakistanis fighting amongst themselves, helping him consolidate his hold over the country.

This is not to suggest that democracy has done much better, for it hasn't. However, research on the Z.A. Bhutto period has shown that it was 'bad luck' more than bad management which resulted in a poor economic performance — the contributing factors being the loss of East Pakistan, a quadrupling of oil prices, and years of pest attacks and floods playing havoc with agricultural production. While corruption, mismanagement and bad governance have had a formidable role to play in the worst period since independence (the eleven years of democracy from 1988-99), there is much consensus amongst economists that adherence, if not capitulation, to IMF's and World Bank's structural adjustment programmes since 1988 may have been a far greater factor. It has always been easier for the elite to borrow from abroad rather than undertake proper adjustment and restructuring measures — why tax your own constituency when you can borrow at cheap rates from international financial institutions?

An excursion into Pakistan's economic history suggests that there are very special conditions which have led to high growth under military dictators and it is not a natural rule or law that suggests that military governments *cause* high growth rates. All those who have high hopes of a revival of the economy, therefore, beware. Secondly, in 1958 and even in 1977, it was far easier to manage Pakistan, its economy and society, than it conceivably is today. One will not only have to address the demons let loose under earlier military rules, but since the nature of Pakistan's society is far different from even twenty-two years ago, new sets of rules to govern society will be needed. Moreover, many of the gains made by civil society over the last eleven years, such as the presence of a free press, cannot now be pushed aside very easily. (When things get bad for Musharraf, as they are likely to, he may want to gag the press, but it will not be as easy for him as it was for Zia.) Also, the global and regional situation is fundamentally quite different from either 1958 (when Ayub took over) or 1977 (when Zia took over), with major consequences on the polity in Pakistan.

Several months into Pakistan's third military coup, the time and space to wait-and-see is fast being replaced with a sense of anxiety and the fear that the military government has little to offer in terms of concrete, focussed and targeted solutions to Pakistan's numerous and well-recognised

*To succeed, Musharraf has to take bold measures but the army seems to be clueless about how to run things.*

problems. There is growing concern that the military government, like all its (civilian) predecessors, is concerned more with goodwill, rhetoric and promises than with any form of concrete action. Moreover, the concrete measures that have been taken in the last few months have produced few, if any, positive results. In fact, some of the moves may actually have very serious negative consequences on investor confidence and on attempts to revive the economy.

There are several reasons why the military government is likely to fail in its attempt to change things around, going by the self-proclaimed chief executive's agenda and the subsequent pronouncements of his team, a strange coterie of people in itself. (It includes NGO activists, well-known economists, educationists and many of the old guard who are always around to help the military and unelected governments.) We will not question the motives or intentions of the military government behind its desire to improve things and will even assume that it is sincere in wanting to achieve what it professes. The trouble is that to implement his ambitious agenda — and to leave his mark on Pakistan — Musharraf will have to take bold and radical measures; marginal changes of the type initiated so far are not going to help. But the military is undecided on how long it will stay and seems to be clueless about how to run things. For several reasons enumerated below, the military's agenda will achieve little in terms of concrete successes, resulting in a desperate and disastrous collapse of the very high expectations that people have from the military government.

There are three main planks to Pakistan's foreign policy which have come to determine the country's domestic, economic and international status and position, and these are responsible for many of the problems that exist in the country. Pakistan's relations with the US, Afghanistan and India determine its relations with the rest of the world, and also have an impact on its domestic situation. The military government's proclamation that 'our foreign policy will remain the same' as in the past, gives a clear indication that it has not thought things through on this front, and has not been able to see the connection between foreign policy and many of the country's problems articulated by Musharraf in his interviews and in his agenda.

Many of us have repeatedly written in newspapers and academic journals that a large number of Pakistan's problems in the past were due to ill-perceived and ill-thought-out foreign policy. The fact that Pakistan is one of only three countries which recognises the Taliban government in Afghanistan should itself be an indication of Pakistan's international isolation. Moreover, the excessive involvement of Pakistan's religious and military establishment in the Taliban 'factor' has had repercussions on civil society in the country. The religious lobbies in Pakistan have been strengthened and emboldened by the successes of their brethren in Afghanistan, and harbour visions of creating Talibanesque societies across Bosnia, Chechnya, Pakistan and Kashmir. The impact of Pakistan's involvement with the Taliban has been felt particularly in the North West Frontier Province, where social, economic, cultural, political and institutional conflicts continue to simmer between Afghani immigrants and the local population.

If Pakistan's previous policy vis-a-vis India and Kashmir is likely to persist, that too does not bode well for Pakistani citizens. After the military's disastrous adventure in Kashmir this spring and summer, one would have hoped for a more rational and progressive policy with respect to India in order to sort out contentious issues once and for all. While the military is and has always been the greatest beneficiary of Pakistan's adventurous and aggressive policy towards India, one would have hoped that now while it has complete authority and control over the country and does not have to compete with a civilian setup for resources or for power, it could have come up with saner statements regarding India, and could have actually worked to resolve issues which have persisted for more than five decades. To retain the status quo regarding India is a great step backwards.

As regards the US, Pakistan has been quite subservient to US interests in the region from the mid-1950s and has never really had an independent foreign policy. Pakistan has to rely on US help because of its dependence on foreign aid — it

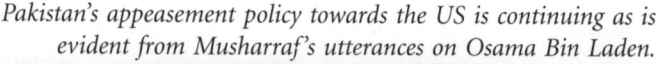

*Pakistan's appeasement policy towards the US is continuing as is evident from Musharraf's utterances on Osama Bin Laden.*

currently owes thirty-two billion dollars, which is forty-seven per cent of its GDP, to institutions such as the World Bank, the IMF and others. In the past, relying on US help also meant being America's frontline state against the former Soviet Union's 'expansionism' in Afghanistan and the region. The appeasement policy is continuing — it appears from Musharraf's utterances that he would not mind getting involved in the US campaign to get Osama Bin Laden, who is America's 'enemy number one' and is in hiding in Afghanistan.

The aggressive and militaristic basis of Pakistan's foreign policy results in bad economics. One key feature of Pakistan's economic policy in the past has been the large share of military expenditure under non-military regimes. Now, with the military itself constituting government, the nature of the 'military' budget becomes a little blurred.

One of the most important planks of the military government, the possibility of a revival of the economy, looks exceedingly bleak, given the fact that the military government will not undertake new measures but continue with the old policies. In Pakistan's case, these policies are mainly those devised and enforced by the IMF and the World Bank.

What has happened to the economy since 1988 is best summarised by a handful of key economic indicators generated by the Government of Pakistan over the last decade. First, the overall growth rate of GDP has fallen well below trend levels, and appreciably below the average of the 1980s. In the eleven years since the implementation of the IMF structural adjustment programme, only once was the GDP growth more than the average six per cent observed since 1977; it was 2.27 per cent in 1992-93 and 1.3 per cent in 1996-97, the lowest in over three decades. Since 1988, inflation was in double digits seven times; in forty years previously, inflation had touched double digits only seven times. Even the State Bank of Pakistan's annual report for 1996-97 admitted that 'it was one of the most difficult and disappointing years in the economic history of the country.' And this was prior to the disastrous policy of the freeze in foreign currency accounts in 1998, after which things only became far worse. These were frozen after Pakistan's nuclear tests in May 1998 to stop a run on the banks. Pakistanis had deposited 11.2 billion dollars in the country's banks — they are legally allowed to open foreign currency accounts — but all this money had been spent by various governments in the past. There was no money to repay these deposit holders, and so the freeze was an inevitability. The step is considered to be one of the most significant events in Pakistan's history and the recent recession is said to have originated from this measure.

Since it is more than probable that the same policies devised by the IMF and the World Bank which were responsible for these downward trends are likely to continue in the future, we have little reason to celebrate. Moreover, under the four democratic regimes since 1988, these policies were, at times, halfheartedly followed through because of their obvious negative consequences, and had to be slowed down or even abandoned due to public pressure and protest. What is worse and more worrisome then is that with little need to be popular as they do not have to face an election, the military government can go all-out to enforce these policies. The eventual consequences are likely to be far different from the expectations of the military or its supporters.

The fact that the government has decided to go ahead with a rise in domestic petrol prices in line with international prices, and extend the scope of the general sales tax is further proof that the economic policy also remains unchanged. Also, the continued reference to 'harsh measures' is preparing the public for worse to come. With investor confidence still very low partly due to the military government's accountability drive, a 'revival' of the economy seems very unlikely.

The one area where the government has already taken some action in its first three months is the one it likes to call 'accountability.' However, this is a misnomer, if ever there was one. By going after bank defaulters the military government has recovered a mere five per cent of bad loans, mainly from politicians and other well-connected businessmen. In its enthusiasm to arrest the corrupt, the military government did not even take the trouble to implement proper foreclosure laws or to bring about measures which would deal with bank defaulters, many of whom are already facing cases in the banking tribunals. By identifying a handful of businessmen/politicians who have taken loans that they have not returned, the government has only made matters far worse.

In an environment where investor confidence is already at 'rock bottom' — the new military government's favourite cliche — indiscriminately going after those who had taken loans has only forced real investors to shy away from expanding their business or to play their part in the process of reviving the economy. In addition, banks with excess liquidity are now also less willing to lend to their clients, as they fear a second round of 'accountability' which will target bank officers who had sanctioned the loans in the past. All this means that attempts to jump-start the economy are likely to fail.

Most important, however, is the military's understanding of the concept of 'accountability.' Bank defaults form only a minuscule element of the term 'accountability,' and going after such defaulters does not either improve the government's fiscal/economic position, nor does it address the nature of the problems that afflict most Pakistanis. If any government was serious and sincere about starting a process of accountability, it should have gone after those who extort money from the lay public or who misuse their governmental positions. The police, the bureaucracy and the judiciary are the bane of the common citizen of Pakistan, and not those who have taken large loans from public sector banks.

The military government has failed in its attempts to hold other than a few individuals 'accountable'. None of the measures taken so far affects the common citizen of Pakistan. In fact, many observers feel that the so-called accountability process started by the military government is merely an attempt to vilify politicians, and that it has no real intention (or is incapable of) starting a proper process of accountability at the lower tiers in the country.

Will the fervour of Musharraf's military government regarding its 'decentralisation' agenda be reminiscent of Zia's zeal for his particular brand of Islamisation? All indications so far seem to suggest so, as growing lip service is paid to this concept by the general himself and by other officials of his military government.

There can be no denying the fact that there is a need for

a substantial, 'radical' restructuring of the state in order to address issues that affect the people, whether in large cities or in remoter rural areas. A thorough and substantive restructuring of the Pakistani state will raise questions about the present administrative boundaries of the provinces — whether there should be only four provinces, or three times that number; whether the concept of an autonomous elected metropolitan government for Pakistan's eight one-million-plus cities can be delayed further; whether the role of commissioners and their deputies in rural areas ought to continue as before; whether the role of the federal government should continue as it does at district level; whether provincial autonomy can be further delayed.

Unfortunately, despite the lip service being paid to the idea of decentralisation, devolution, etc., all indications suggest that the military government cannot (or will not) take 'radical' and structural measures. Discussions with those who are in a position to propose policies and implement them reveal that they feel they 'do not have the luxury of time' to implement any substantive changes. If that is how this military government feels, that indeed is a lost opportunity.

What this means then is that the military government will, at best, propose some changes in existing laws (perhaps in the local government ordinance of 1979), but little else. The local government ordinances of the four provinces were promulgated twenty years ago under a martial law government. The economic, social, demographic and particularly, political conditions under which those ordinances were framed, are very different to the nature of Pakistani society in 1999. Clearly, only the fine-tuning of an outdated model will solve few of the problems that exist. The military government's half-hearted attempts at decentralisation, therefore, may follow the same pattern as the Islamisation programme of Pakistan's last military dictator.

B y adopting a modern, secular, liberal, modern façade, the military has been smart enough to co-opt a large number of individuals into positions of government from that thing called 'civil' society. (Can one still call it 'civil' society when it not only endorses but actually joins, *uncivil* society, i.e. the military?) Many liberals and democrats (at least one thought that this is what they were) have jumped onto the bandwagon and accepted positions of prominence as ministers at the federal and provincial level, while others are active behind the scenes, assisting or advising government and waiting to be asked to join government at a more formal level. Sadly, not too many of those from 'civil' society now in high office would have been willing to work with previous (elected) governments. It has become increasingly difficult to find individuals who feel that despite the 'sham' or poor democratic showing in Pakistan since 1985, the process of democracy should have been allowed to continue.

The liberal intelligentsia and the elite see Musharraf as nothing less than a saviour, their messiah on a white horse. They feel that Pakistan was never a democracy, and have supported the dismissal of each and every one of the five elected governments since 1988. This section of Pakistan's privileged class is more concerned with 'good governance,' swift and fair justice, the end of nepotism and corruption, and a revival of the economy. It matters not how these goals are achieved, as long as someone fulfils them. All these have been promised by

Pakistan's new chief executive, and hence the unflinching support for him. A benevolent dictator, it is argued, is far better than a despotic, incompetent and corrupt democratically elected leader. In all this, they forget that 'good governance' requires participation, pluralism, accountability and openness, none of which can form part of undemocratic military rule, no matter how benevolent.

All those liberals who are banking on the military are the very same ones who backed the World Bank's Moeen Quereshi when he was a caretaker prime minister for three months in 1993. This time, they are openly stating that they want the military to stay for some time, two years at least, so that it can cleanse the democratic stables of their undemocratic components. They are relieved that the chief of the army staff does not wear a beard and speak the language of Zia or the Taliban. But this, precisely, is the problem. By supporting this intrusion by the military in Pakistan's politics, next time round they may get the worst end of the stick. It is this liberal and supposedly pro-democratic element which has probably done Pakistan its biggest disservice. Had they been an active and effective lobby in the first place, things would not have come to the stage where they have. Pakistan's greatest tragedy regarding democracy is not that the military has taken over, but that its people allowed democracy to degenerate to the level it did, and for that to happen in the first place.

For those of us who do not have much faith in the ability of the military government to enforce substantive and far-reaching structural changes in Pakistan's foreign and economic policies, or to initiate measures to restructure the very character of the state itself (which by its very nature would undermine the status, role and position of the military), the choices are far too few. For the very few members of 'civil' society who are not as yet in, or with, the military government, this is the time to take stock of what constitutes 'civil' society especially now that it has joined uncivil society. In addition, this is also an appropriate moment to propose alternative visions for Pakistan, regarding its economic and foreign policies, decentralisation, accountability, matters of law and justice, and a host of other areas and disciplines which need to be redefined. All of these measures, however, require political action. One of the major shortcomings of 'civil' society in Pakistan in the past has been its lack of engagement with broader political issues, and more specifically, with political parties. For those of us who are still part of that small group which would continue to call itself 'civil', perhaps there could be no better opportunity to realise that it is crucial that civil society embraces political society and begins to play a role worthy of its name.

# March of the Generals

## AZIZ SIDDIQUI

Pakistanis have alternately embraced civilian and military rule just because of their successive let-downs, says the joint director of the human rights commission of Pakistan. And now they have no choice but to heave that democratic stone uphill yet again.

U ntil his fall, Mian Nawaz Sharif had seemed to have a sort of Midas touch in reverse. He handled no challenge, real or imagined, that he did not turn to dust: the presidency and the judiciary, parliament, political allies as well as the Opposition, the media, the bureaucracy and the Opposition-majority province. He even boasted of this prowess in parliament, to warn future challengers. This was soon after what had seemed like the ultimate triumph, when he had worsted the army chief of the time, Jahangir Karamat, himself. Later, his devotees saw his magic at work even in his downfall. 'See, the bounder has proved lucky again,' said one long-time loyalist. 'The army got him before the people could.'

It remains to be seen how that 'luck' holds through the anti-terrorist court and the other courts to follow where he faces multiple jeopardy. If it is not hijacking and treason, it will be attempted murder. If not that, corruption. And there will always be the so-called law of necessity for his prosecutors to fall back on — that the good of the people is the supreme law, etc. — which authenticated at least two of the past three military coups.

As of now, it seems even this luckiest of politicians had to go dig his own grave. The army here wasn't, historically, sworn to abstinence. It had had a record of being edgy. It had to be afforded no excuse to come in, much less an excuse of a kind that would make many people acclaim its coming.

It all looks despairingly like the curse of Sisyphus. The country huffs and puffs to heave the democratic stone uphill. Soon the direction goes awry. The effort becomes too much. In one fell movement the stone comes rolling all the way back to the bottom. And then the exertion has to begin all over again.

Is the country doomed to this Sisyphean chore?

The disincentives for army intervention could not have been greater this time round. Forget the notional virtues of democracy. Forget even the demonstrated ravages of military rules around the world — even recently, from Chile to Nigeria to Indonesia. More relevantly, the expedient usefulness of a dictator to the big power game had ended with the Cold War. The stability and the assurance of unquestioning partnership that the dictator had promised to outsiders was no longer a pressing, overriding need. An usurper in uniform, therefore, was very unlikely now to find obliging patrons among the rich abroad.

Equally relevant were the dampeners at home. The military rulers of the past — Ayub Khan, Yahya Khan and Zia ul-Haq — might have come in to the beat of drums. But they all had to go amid boos and catcalls or worse. (Not that the civilian elected rulers have had any warmer farewells, but that's another story.)

Then, considering the desperate straits of the economy and the raft of all the other problems pressing hard on all sides, what could the army do after seizing power anyway? It could look forward only to the briefest of honeymoons. Was it such a bad choice then to stay in the background, to keep pulling whatever strings were necessary to pull, and let others take all the flak of non-performance, rather than go and seize momentary pomp and power and take all the blame itself?

I s military intervention in this country, then, a compulsive act, born of some manufacturing fault, or some ethnic or religious dysfunction, or a distortion at birth in the military's own mindset?

Impatience with democratic methods is not, of course, a Pakistani peculiarity, nor one exclusive to Muslim states. Those who have had the running of this country have not been devout Muslims anyway. Several other countries have been beset with similar or worse problems, without the military butting in every now and again and taking charge. It's true that the military, almost everywhere, is trained to view things as black or white, regard people as friends or foes, see action in terms of command and compliance. Like fundamentalists of all hues, they also have a sense of immutability about things, and a single-mindedness in the drive towards appointed objectives. But in most cases, they also often learn to remain within their allotted parameters.

The peculiarities of Pakistan have lain not just in the acuteness of flaws in its polity, but also in the ineffectiveness of countervailing checks. Three more or less interlinked features particularly stand out: the unusual objective circumstances of the country's birth; the preeminence the military acquired almost from the start; and the extraordinary obstreperousness with which the game of politics came to be played in Pakistan.

The country was unique in that it comprised two far-flung parts, East and West Pakistan, divided by the whole breadth of India. The people on the two sides virtually had nothing in common except mostly their religion and an initial untested allegiance to common nationhood and statehood. The resources were so meagre that almost within months of independence the finance minister had to send an SOS abroad for financial assistance. The ruling Muslim League party had been the weakest in the areas that made Pakistan. And the hard core of talent in various other sectors, poor as it was, was very thinly spread.

With all that, the country had to start at the deep end. It was faced with a two-way movement of a devastated population — the massive influx of Muslim refugees from India and the outflow from Pakistan of Hindu talent and enterprise. To these were added the problems of relations with India which got off to a bad start, and grew worse with time. Early hiccups occurred in the division of assets (causing Gandhiji himself to go on a fast), the share of defence materiel, the movement of troops on the borders, the apportionment of Indus waters and, of course, the fighting over Kashmir. All that contributed to the perception here of a lasting threat from a giant neighbour forever angered by, and unreconciled to, an integral part breaking away from it.

Most of the India-Pakistan problems were a carry-over from the past or a direct consequence of Partition. They were not unusual in the circumstances. They should have mellowed with time, especially since they were largely born of distrust, real or imagined wrongs, and the communal-cum-political polarisation of pre-independence years. Time and mounting compulsions for cooperation were certain to progressively dilute the bitterness just as they did elsewhere in the world. But the standing sore of Jammu & Kashmir kept befouling the atmosphere and queering the pitch for any advance of that natural healing process.

The popular Pakistani view even outside of the military and governmental circles has been of having been wronged on Jammu & Kashmir. Given the state's circumstances, the terms of independence dictated self-determination by the people whether to join one successor country or the other. The United

*The popular Pakistani view even outside of the military and government circles has been of having been wronged on Kashmir.*

Nations mandated it too. And the leaderships of the two countries had also pledged themselves to it. That seemed the fundamental, irreducible element of the issue. Various Pakistani governments might have committed a series of follies to force a breakthrough but that did not, in the people's perception, cancel out or mitigate the basic injustice.

It is this problem with India that gave and continues to give to the military its abiding preeminence in the public eye despite the extraordinary cost it manifestly imposes on the national resources and despite the people's subsequent disenchantment with its recurrent assumption of a political role.

The military isn't, of course, seen as a likely instrument of an eventual conquest of Kashmir. If there were any such illusions they were for the most part dispelled as one war followed another. There were few military landmarks to fill the nation with pride. The 1965 war, apart from individual feats, long ceased to be regarded as an hour of national glory. And the shame of the 1971 conflict was so overwhelming it has been sought to be blotted from national memory. The findings of the Hamoodur Rehman Inquiry Commission that went into the causes and conduct of that war have remained a state secret all these years. That attempt to protect the military's image was obviously futile.

The armed forces are nevertheless an essential token of strength. Mere possession of that strength, and not necessarily the exercise of it, is considered important to sustain a claim, even if that has to be done at great cost and against a much stronger neighbour. The military is believed to provide a sense of security in the face of the tension that must in any case follow from the maintenance and continuous assertion of that claim. There is perhaps an awkward practical logic to this. The world is replete with examples where, if a country was manifestly weak, even its just and long-standing grievance against a neighbour progressively died on its feet and the status quo quickly became a given of history. Many Pakistanis may still be willing to go a long way to prevent that from happening to Kashmir.

It does not, of course, suit powerful interests in the country to recognise that a nation's strength does not come just from the size of its military, but even more from the wellbeing of its people. And it requires a level of maturity unfortunately lacking, varyingly, in both countries to see that mutual cooperation may just succeed in eventually delivering an acceptable settlement of disputes where confrontation has so manifestly failed; that it at least deserves an honest chance.

Thus, the military became, over time, the foremost guardian of the state, the guarantor of its existence. What was good for it was good for the country. The foreign policy began to be shaped in the light of the needs of the military, and domestic policies were influenced by foreign ties and the counsels of the defence forces.

T he first military putsch against the government — which, as it turned out, was never very seriously meant — was thought of as early as 1950 at the time of Liaquat

*The first military coup was thought of as early as 1950 at the time of Liaquat Ali Khan, Pakistan's first prime minister, and the trigger was Kashmir.*

Ali Khan, the country's first prime minister. The trigger was reputedly Kashmir, the putschists said to be favouring a military solution to the issue. The latter were headed by Maj. Gen. Akbar Khan, a popular figure, who was then being proposed for the post of commander-in-chief.

As diplomatic papers released later have shown, it was more of a frame-up. Rivalries within the army between the Akbar Khan group, which favoured a more independent foreign policy, and the other headed by the pro-Anglo-American Maj. Gen. Ayub Khan, caused some insignificant exchanges and meetings to be magnified to seem like an imminent plot. It enabled the latter group to eliminate the challenge of the other, and later to induce a crackdown on communist and all left-leaning elements in the country. (It also enabled Ayub Khan rather than Akbar Khan to get promoted as the C-in-C.)

The proceedings of the tribunal that tried these eleven military officers and four civilians were never made public. One of those civilians was the famed Urdu poet Faiz Ahmad Faiz, who then had to spend four years in jail. About the so-called conspiracy he wrote the memorable lines: *Woh baat saray fasanay mein jiska zikr nahin / Woh baat unhein bahut nagwar guzri hai.*

Differences in the first Cabinet of Liaquat Ali Khan similarly occurred from security considerations, such as whether or not Pakistan should play a direct role in the fighting in Kashmir, and later whether Pakistan should make its support to the US in the Korean war conditional on supply of American arms to it. Finance Minister Ghulam Mohammed, later to become governor-general, was said to have dubbed the Cabinet as a 'stable with mules', and once tartly asked Prime Minister Liaquat Ali to 'govern or get out'.

Liaquat Ali's official visit to the US in May 1950 (made in preference to a prior invitation from the Soviet Union), when he also had a special session in the Pentagon, was primarily devoted to convincing Washington of the strategic importance to it of Pakistan's friendship and of the need for Pakistan being quickly and suitably armed. An Islamic state, he ardently argued, could only be as strongly opposed to communism as the US was. To the Americans of those days no allurement could be more irresistible.

The first national commander-in-chief, Ayub Khan, also soon began to see it as his responsibility not only to guide the government on military matters but to counsel it on foreign policy and even domestic issues. He began to develop ideas on politics and statecraft too.

His being made a Cabinet minister in 1954 in a way set a public seal on the involvement in politics of the army's brass, if not of the army as such. And it also shifted the tilt of the state structure: from being political to being military-bureaucratic. The Constituent Assembly had just rejected the proposal of merging the provinces of the western wing into one unit; passed constitutional amendments that stripped the governor-general of the powers of dismissing the Cabinet; and accorded the assembly members certain immunity. This was seen as a coup of sorts against Punjab and the governor-general.

The governor-general, Ghulam Mohammed, then rallied, dissolved the Constituent Assembly and swore in a so-called Cabinet of talent. Among these, there were three key figures: the C-in-C, Gen. Ayub Khan, became defence minister; defence secretary Maj. Gen. Iskander Mirza was inducted as minister of interior; and Chaudhri Mohammad Ali, considered a strong representative of the civil service and of Punjab, continued as finance minister.

The alignment with the Anglo-American bloc was then formalised and a succession of military pacts were entered into. Bilateral relations and internal policies were adapted so as to be compatible with the alignment to the principal superpower. All this was primarily driven by military-bureaucratic rather than political considerations. The military and the bureaucracy now became the dominant elements of governance.

Except for the first one that was aborted at birth, military coups were not prompted by strategic considerations. Ayub or Yahya, Zia or now Musharraf did not press a plea of defence failure or external threat among their reasons for intervention. They could not do that since they had had a decisive say in these matters — nor these alone — even when not in political power. They came in because they thought there was a mess no one else could cope with. They stayed on because they believed they were doing a better job of governing than others. Personal ambition must also, though, have often played a part. The feel of the trigger can be heady. When the trigger is held in monopoly, the feeling can climb an extra notch or two if restraints, personal or institutional, are easy to bend.

Ayub Khan had, by his own account, started reflecting early on how political restructuring needed to be done. He felt impatient with the messy ways of the politicians, and also thought that the Westminster style of government did not suit the hot climate and the 'genius' of the people in Pakistan.

During a visit to London in 1954, Ayub had paced his

Dorchester Hotel room to produce what he called 'A Short Appreciation of Present and Future Problems of Pakistan.' That had included the blueprint of so-called 'basic democracies' which he was later as the country's self-appointed president to impose on the country.

This 'basic democracies' were a five-tier structure comprising the directly-elected union councils at the grassroots, superimposed by the tehsil, district, division and provincial councils. Ayub also found a soulmate in Iskander Mirza who was himself staunchly of the conviction that the country could only be governed through what he called a 'controlled democracy'. Mirza, originally from Murshidabad, was a military officer turned civil servant. His entrée into the upper reaches of governance began with his appointment as governor of East Pakistan with full powers following the ouster of the two-month-old elected government of Moulvi Fazlul Haq and imposition of governor's rule there in 1954. After that there was hardly a political intrigue at the high levels of which Mirza was not a part.

The conditions became ripe to strike for the Ayub-Mirza duo around mid-1958 when the politicians were presenting — and being manipulated, mostly by Mirza, to present — a rugby ground melee. The country's first general election scheduled to be held early the following year also threatened to reduce the space for these behind-the-scene operators. There followed three prime ministers of three different political parties in the space of two years — Husseyn Shaheed Suhrawardy of Awami League led his coalition from September 1956 to October 1957; I.I. Chundrigar of Muslim

League lasted for just two months; followed by Feroz Khan Noon of the Mirza-sponsored Republican Party.

Mirza and Ayub felt they had now to step in, and in one fell swoop they swept the deck clean. They dismissed the Noon government, dissolved the assemblies, abrogated the Constitution and imposed martial law. This was also quickly followed by internal attrition. Iskander Mirza himself had to be disposed of since the military, naturally enough, wished to have the deck all to itself. He, with his Iranian-born wife Naheed, was put on a plane to London where he spent the remaining few years of his life in obscurity.

Gen. Yahya Khan, C-in-C in 1969, headed the next martial law of that year. He had come in as a result of public agitation against Ayub Khan's prolonged military rule. Ayub, promoted as field marshal during his presidency, had taken on a civilian, elective and constitutional garb in the later part of his rule, but that did not much alter the nature of his governance and people hankered for a more democratic and federal order.

Yahya had to promise to be there just to oversee the transition to the democratic order, while no doubt quietly hoping to carve a niche for himself in the new setup. In the event, he had to go in a hurry because of the defeat in the 1971 war with India.

T he deeper and lasting consequences of the spells of direct military rule took time to sink, but when they did sink the reaction was fairly widespread. How is it then that the military has kept getting the initial welcome it usually has? Pakistanis have rather been in the position of the rustic who, offered the choice between two categories of punishments, kept fleeing from the rigours of one to the other, and then back, until he ended up undergoing the full measure of both. Pakistanis have alternately embraced the civilian and military rules with about equal gusto just because of their successive disenchantments. It has been the push-, rather than the pull-factor, that has been more operative.

The democratic form has, of course, its normal handicaps. Its performance is slow, noisy and relatively inefficient; it makes corruption a little more difficult to hide; and it has to keep negotiating for popular support which may not always be by fair means. All of which are multiplied in the early stages of democratic development when traditions of fairplay have not been formed and institutions of accountability are not strong.

The democratic experiment in Pakistan has had a further, even more decisive, faultline. The military's looming presence in politics from almost the start, and later the precedent of its direct assumption of power, has had a distortional, even a destabilising, influence on almost every stage of the process. Every civilian government has had to reckon with the possibility of the military playing favourites behind the scenes, even of its contemplating a direct intercession. The former has had to keep itself open to the latter's wishes, try to create loyalties for itself, and, when possible, try and build safeguards for itself.

Consider a few latter-day examples of the military's political outreach and the distortions it might have caused: In the 1988 general election, the anti-PPP alliance of all the right-wing parties, called the Islami Jamhoori Ittehad (Islamic Democratic Alliance), and led by Muslim League, was formed at the behest and with the blandishments of the ISI. The ISI chief of the time, Gen. Hamid Gul, admitted this later arguing that there was nothing wrong with it, that he was working for a national cause.

The organisation did not confine itself just to political persuasion. It doled out vast sums of money to the contesting political parties it thought it could gain a handle on and which it wanted to win seats in the assemblies. When another retired ISI chief spilled the beans, a few of the beneficiaries had to acknowledge the largesse received, and even the army chief of that time, Gen. Mirza Aslam Beg, had to later admit to the transaction though he claimed that the army itself had had no part in it. Air Marshal Asghar Khan's petition against the interference by a military institution in the political process has been pending in the Supreme Court for two years.

When despite ISI's exertion, the People's Party managed to win a plurality of seats in the 1988 parliament, the president did not automatically invite the party head, Benazir Bhutto, to form a government and prove her majority support, as required by the Constitution. He dithered. Benazir had first to go and be interviewed by the then chief of army staff, Mirza Aslam Beg and, it is commonly believed, was made to agree to a set of conditions before the army chief gave a nod to the president. The conditions were said to include her non-interference in military's affairs, ditto with the nuclear programme, wariness in relations with India, and no settling of political scores by her.

Apart from the real or induced weaknesses of civilian governments and the strength of the military's self-belief, the factor that greatly eased the procession of generals in the governing of the country was the role of the judiciary.

In October 1954, Governor-General Ghulam Mohammed dissolved the first Constituent Assembly as a backlash to the assembly's adopting a constitutional amendment to render the actions of the governor-general subject to the advice of the Cabinet. After nine months of legal wrangling the action was struck down as unconstitutional by the Sindh high court. The government then made sure beforehand that its appeal to the federal court would be upheld and the assembly would stay dissolved.

Messages were exchanged between the governor-general and Chief Justice Mohammad Munir and the latter later admitted in his memoirs that the assembly speaker, Maulvi Tamizuddin Khan, had lost the case the very first day that he entered the courtroom. In the event, the appeal was upheld not on the merit of the case but on a pure technicality; even whose legality remains seriously questioned in subsequent legal commentaries.

Similarly, Iskander Mirza and Ayub Khan's abrogation of the Constitution; dissolution of the assembly and imposition of martial law in 1958 was upheld by the supreme judiciary on the grounds of the welfare of the people and of the republic being the supreme law. That virtually dispensed with the need for any reference to a law or the Constitution. It left it to the courts to decide if the demands of the welfare of the people as portrayed by the state lawyers were indeed such as to have left the coup-makers with no choice but to intervene.

The same principle was applied over Zia's assumption of power in 1977. The court not only endorsed the action on the basis of the supposed law of necessity but it also permitted the new government to make any changes it thought necessary in the Constitution, since care was taken this time not to abrogate the Constitution but only to 'suspend' it in several parts.

The only occasions when the judiciary ruled against the military chief's action was when the judgement was relevant only for the record. On the arrest of a political figure Malik Ghulam Jilani Malik early in 1971, a habeas corpus and bail petition was moved in the Lahore high court. Dismissing the petition for lack of jurisdiction the court said that the courts were barred from challenging the martial law orders. The Supreme Court then took on the appeal in a landmark constitutional case in 1972.

The court ruled in this famous Asma Jilani case that Yahya Khan had, in fact, usurped power in 1969, that his action was not justified by the doctrine of revolutionary legality, and therefore his martial law regime had been illegal. But at the time of that unusual judgement that regime had already, for several months, been part of history.

That judgement was allowed to have no bearing on the decision on the subsequent coup staged by Zia. Later, in 1988, Zia's ouster of another elected government, that of Mohammad Khan Junejo, was again held illegal. Again, by then, Zia was dead and buried. The court did not, however, follow it up with the logical step of restoring the Junejo government. The army chief of the time, Mirza Aslam Beg, claimed afterwards that that was not done on *his* advice, because he wanted the election process already underway to run its course.

*A new chief justice is sworn in in Pakistan as the sitting chief justice refuses to pledge allegiance to Musharraf's provisional constitutional order.*

The legality of Musharraf's coup is now under challenge in the courts. Apparently, there was uncertainty in the official mind if, as in the cases of Ayub and Zia, the present judiciary too would admit the principle of 'revolutionary legality' or the 'law of necessity' and validate the present coup. There was a danger that it could instead lean on its original oath to uphold the Constitution and thus declare the act to have been unconstitutional.

Just a few days before the hearing of the case was to begin in the Supreme Court, an order was issued requiring all the judges of the superior courts to take a fresh oath. Under this oath they had to pledge allegiance not to the constitution (which the coup had declared suspended) but to the first provisional constitutional order (PCO-1) which Musharraf had issued after taking over. While under the suspended Constitution any coup would be an offence of the first order, under PCO-1 it was a questioning of any of the chief executive's acts by any court that was impermissible.

It was Zia who had set the precedent of subjecting the judiciary to a solemn affirmation of compliance to a provisional constitution of his making, one which stripped the judiciary itself of its critical powers. The ploy was also used, then as now, to get rid of unwanted judges by simply not inviting them to the new swearing in. Some others also, again then as now, themselves opted out by just not agreeing to this extra-constitutional revision of their remit. This toll of the judges added up to ten in Zia's exercise, to thirteen in the present one.

Late Justice Dorab Patel, one of the most distinguished and independent jurists to adorn the bench, had once summed up the judiciary's dilemma at times like these in plain words. If there was no stir among the people outside, he had said, you couldn't expect five men sitting inside a courtroom to give a ruling against martial law.

The future of democracy in this country looks nearly as uncertain as its past has been rocky. The principle challenges the democratic process faces seem on past record likely to stay unresolved over the foreseeable future. As long as relations with India remain on a knife's edge, pre-eminence of the armed forces and the drain on national resources will continue. The military will also continue to be cast, and to cast itself, in the role of the defender not only of territorial but also of so-called ideological frontiers. (The reverse of this may also in part be true.)

Secondly, given the state of the national economy, the ship of the state is certain to keep making heavy weather of it and keep sailing now and again into a maelstrom. No government, civilian or military, can long delay a sharp slide into unpopularity.

Thirdly, levels of democratic and federal underdevelopment will not make governance easy. Governments will be even more prone to committing follies (such as bending to or even encouraging religious fundamentalism) and thus making their problems become even worse confounded. The bedrock of democratic government will also be hard to create in circumstances where cutting legal and constitutional corners in the name of national interest has been common, and where the judiciary hasn't earned a reputation for blowing the whistle on government's playing foul.

Any change will have to begin at the popular level. It may be a cliché, but in the end not even the military is stronger than the people. The print media and the activist NGOs will need to ensure that they remain free and active. They need to strengthen civil society and help it become better informed, better organised and more articulate.

No dictator, elected or self-imposing, should thrive on the basis that the majority is silent or acquiescent or is fooled by shows of reformist fervour. Sickened by Milosevic's propaganda, groups of Serbians once started the practice of coming out of their houses with empty pots and pans at the time of the main TV news and beating them hard and loud as long as the bulletin lasted. People have to find collective non-violent ways of demonstrating their displeasure, rather than sulk in silence or find catharsis in mutual grumbling.

Secondly, political parties need to learn the hard lessons from this wholly avoidable disruption of the political process. The PML should recognise why despite the so-called heavy mandate it had received in the election, the unconstitutional toppling of its government was welcomed by the people at large, and it barely raised more than a polite whimper in its own ranks.

It has been said, half in jest, that Allah, the army and America are the dominant elements of Pakistan's make-up. The army, sure enough, is ascendant again. America is perhaps even more of an underwriter of first and last resort now, given Pakistan's increased dependence on it for economic and diplomatic support. And accusatory fundamentalism, which claims to speak on behalf of Allah, looms not far in the background, biding its time.

The challenge is to insert a fourth 'A', Awam, as an axis to those coordinates, and as a corrective to them. The effort then must turn yet again to heaving that Sisyphean stone uphill.

# Fundamental Flaws

## KHALED AHMED

Most secularists in Pakistan see General Musharraf's government as the country's last defence against its Talibanisation, says the consulting editor of the *Friday Times*, Lahore.

Most secularists in Pakistan see Gen. Pervez Musharraf's government as the country's last defence against its Talibanisation. Their fear is that if Musharraf fails, the fundamentalists are bound to take over the country.

Already, Musharraf sits uncomfortably on top of an army that has been indoctrinated with the idea of Islamic jehad over the last two decades. After the death of Gen. Zia ul-Haq in 1988 in an air crash, the half-a-million strong army, spending six per cent of the country's GDP, aroused fears in an establishment that had inherited the Islamic state. There were too many Islamist generals in the running for the top job, committed to the principle of international jehad. In 1990, an adventurist army chief, Gen. Aslam Beg, was gotten rid of just before he

*Musharraf already sits uncomfortably on top of a jehadised army and does not want to make things worse for himself by aligning openly with the Islamists.*

could stage a coup 'in defiance of American hegemony.' The next chief, Gen. Asif Nawaz, was selected on the basis of his 'professionalism', a euphemism applied to 'secular' officers not attracted to Islamic irredentism abroad and militarist Sharia at home. Asif Nawaz was preferred over the great Islamist ex-chief of the ISI, Gen. Hamid Gul, who never accepted the new leadership in the GHQ.

Asif Nawaz then began the task of purging the Islamist generals from the army's top echelons. He prematurely retired Gen. Hamid Gul for insubordination, and sidelined a number of other Islamists, including Maj. Gen. Zaheerul Islam Abbasi, who retaliated in October 1995 by trying to stage an Islamic 'revolution' in the GHQ 'because he had been made to salute American officers' while on duty in Gilgit.

In 1993, a frightened caretaker government had removed Gen. Javed Nasir as chief of the ISI, put there by Nawaz Sharif, after a senseless act of sabotage in Mumbai without 'clearing it' with the prime minister. In 1997, however, the ISI got Nawaz Sharif to appoint Javed Nasir as chief of Lahore's Auqaf Department, from where he encouraged Sikh irredentism in East Punjab by setting up a Shiromani Gurudwara Prabandhak Committee 'in exile,' even as Nawaz Sharif embraced Atal Behari Vajpayee in Lahore.

Asif Nawaz died in office of a heart attack while under pressure from Islamist ex-army officers employed by Prime Minister Nawaz Sharif in the Intelligence Bureau. But thanks to Asif Nawaz's earlier purge, Gen. Jehangir Karamat, another secular-professional officer, took over as the army chief in 1996. The army was, however, still heavily manned by Islamist officers — the proof came when Karamat's own army journal, *Hilal,* published an editorial against him 'for secularising the army.'

That he was unable to fire or sideline the senior officer who had got the editorial written signalled his weakness as a secular man in the middle of an Islamised organisation. Around this time, Gen. Zaheerul Islam Abbasi, undergoing his sentence in a jail in Haripur Hazara after an unsuccessful attempt to eliminate the 'professional' leadership of the GHQ and declare himself Amirul Momineen — the title assumed earlier by Afghanistan's Taliban leader, Mullah Umar — became the darling of the religious parties, and regularly spirited out his Islamic 'messages' to the Urdu press.

It was Karamat's fear of his own army that made him back down from a confrontation with Nawaz Sharif in 1997 when the latter fired President Farooq Ahmad Khan Leghari and replaced him with a Deobandi ex-judge of the Supreme Court, Muhammad Rafiq Tarar. The jehad in Afghanistan and Kashmir had 'turned Deobandi' and the institutions in Pakistan were stiffening their ideological outlook in anticipation of the new order. Nawaz Sharif was promising a more Islamised society under his 15th Amendment 'Sharia' Bill.

On 12 October 1999, when Musharraf staged his coup against Nawaz Sharif, he had done so against a prime minister who was seen to have betrayed the Islamic jehad in Kashmir and who had expressed dissatisfaction with the 1994 pro-Taliban policy in Afghanistan. All the religious parties, led by the Deobandis and their jehadi off-shoots, had been rearing to begin a revolt against a pro-India and pro-Washington prime minister determined to choke off the financial pipeline that had made them strong and kept them going. It would have been natural for an army chief who had mounted

*When Musharraf said Turkish leader Ataturk was his role model, he got a mouthful from Qazi Hussain Ahmad of Jamaat-e-Islami.*

the Kargil operation to pose as the champion of the religious parties and their jehadi militias, but Musharraf decided against it. And thereby hangs a tale — he knew that if he began the process of aligning the army openly with the Islamists, his own leadership in the GHQ would be imperilled.

In fact, in the run-up to the October 1999 coup, the religious parties were expecting to receive positive high-level messages from the army through military intelligence, but these did not come. The leader of the Jamaat-e-Islami, Qazi Hussain Ahmad, complained in private to a senior journalist in Lahore that the messages which had finally come had emanated from such a low level that they actually encouraged the impression that Musharraf wanted 'to go it alone'. Maulana Akram Awan, Pakistan's most aggressive religious leader whose party, Tanzeem al-Ikhwan, was once credited with having made the deepest penetration into the army, actually decided to join up with Nawaz Sharif after waiting in vain to get a positive signal from the army in response to his outspoken support of Musharraf and his Kargil operation.

Instead, Musharraf, as chief executive of Pakistan, declared that his role model would be the great Turkish secularist reformer, Mustafa Kemal Ataturk. The religious parties were shocked into silence. Only Qazi Hussain Ahmad of Jamaat-e-Islami defied him during a public meeting in Peshawar saying, 'How can Ataturk, who destroyed the Islamic ideology, be the ideal of a Pakistani ruler? Those who are giving such senseless statements to make God angry and America happy should learn a lesson from the fate of Nawaz Sharif.' The next day, Qazi's entry into the North West Frontier Province was banned for a month. A clear message had gone out to the Islamists from the GHQ, but presumably not without a shiver inside the army itself.

Ataturk had been admired by the founder of Pakistan, Mohammed Ali Jinnah. The first book he gave his daughter Dina in the 1930s was a biography of the Grey Wolf. Poet Muhammad Iqbal, considered the 'philosopher of the state' in Pakistan, had supported the secular experiment of Ataturk in Turkey in his famous 1929 English Lectures. In the post-General Zia period in the 1990s, the establishment had reinterpreted Jinnah as an Islamist who wanted the Sharia imposed in Pakistan. And the Iqbal Academy in Lahore had promoted new research pointing to the 'error' of Iqbal in supporting Ataturk's secularism, emphasising the poet's Urdu verse instead where he had actually condemned the Turkish leader.

Musharraf went on to choose his National Security Council and Cabinet from among people known for their 'pragmatic' outlook or their anti-fundamentalist point of view. His discontinuation of the policy of hounding the secular NGOs unshackled the expression of an alternative model for Pakistan. One of Musharraf's ministers, Umar Asghar Khan, is the son of Air Marshall (Retd.) Asghar Khan, who had gone to the Supreme Court against the ISI and publicly called for its disbanding. Umar heads an environmentalist NGO and was being hounded by the NWFP clergy for un-Islamic activities just before his inclusion in the Cabinet. The disheartened intellectual came out of his isolation to appeal for the roll-back of the ideological state to allow breathing space for civil society. Musharraf thus created a space from where support for his 'reluctant' martial law could emerge.

Amid all this, the Islamists were in a state of shock, their jehadi militias still fitfully engaged in Kashmir. But Musharraf shored up rightwing support by reinforcing the state's anti-India stance and allowing the jehad in Kashmir to go up a few notches as a follow-up of the Kargil operation. The support of the Pakistani intellectual got him crucial political concessions in the West despite laws that prevented the US, the European Union and the Commonwealth to help him financially. Above all, the state of the economy persuaded the elite in Pakistan to reinterpret the politics of the nuclear tests of 1998 and see the harm militarisation had done to Pakistan. It appeared to them that an army which had traditionally blocked all initiatives to break Pakistan's security paradigm would now relent in the face of the grave economic crisis and allow for the 'breathing time' the economists had been demanding throughout the 1990s.

The chief executive, however, unleashed a battery of contradictory signals which remain difficult to interpret: how can the army cope with economic reforms that curtail its own agenda; how can it cope with a post-Kargil international opinion which is for removing the army from centrestage in Pakistan; and how can it allow a loosening of the ideological and security paradigm of confrontation with India, simply to gain some economic concessions?

The rumour machine in Pakistan was working overtime in December 1999 as Nawaz Sharif went on trial in a Karachi special anti-terrorism court for trying to hijack Musharraf's plane. The Muslim League was feverishly trying to 'adjust' itself to possible new decisions that Musharraf would make to bail himself out of a possible no-exit situation created by his 'secular' revolt. The rumour was that the two new personal secretaries appointed by him at the GHQ were Ahmedis. A cleric raised the voice of protest in the Urdu press about this unforgivable violation of the country's code of hatred, the sort enforced against the Bahai's in Iran and against the Armenians in Turkey of yore.

The rumour was that Musharraf's bearded chief of general staff, General Aziz, was a Tablighi Islamist, an ex-ISI officer who had played a central role in the Kargil operation and who was probably responsible for getting his co-believer in the Deobandi faith, Gen. Javed Nasir, posted to the Auqaf Department in Lahore from where to organise an irredentist Khalistan movement against India (the religious properties of the Sikhs in Punjab are handled by Auqaf Department). Another rumour was that General Usmani in Karachi, who had played a pivotal role in saving Musharraf from Nawaz Sharif's hijack adventure, was also a bearded Deobandi-Tablighi officer. The secular behaviour of the chief executive couldn't have gone down well with these key officers.

It was concluded by those reading the tea-leaves of the chief executive's hidden agenda that he might bow out of power in the face of the growing Western demand that he switch off the forward policy on Kashmir and settle with India, and that he change the past policy of supporting the Taliban in Afghanistan. Musharraf's initiative of calling in Awami National Party's secretary-general, Ajmal Khatak, for 'discussions' was interpreted as a testing of political waters before handing over the reins to an interim civilian government. The Muslim League's senior vice-president and General Zia's son, Ijazul Haq, immediately floated his 'formula', offering to ditch Nawaz Sharif and his kitchen cabinet in return for a restoration of the assemblies, meaning that the Muslim League would purge Nawaz Sharif and do the bidding of the GHQ.

Musharraf denied having any plans of a hand-over to 'selected' politicians, but the denial was not taken seriously by the politicians. Seeing that Musharraf was secular in outlook or at least neutral in religion, the right-wing elements, backed by Islamabad's Council of Islamic Ideology, raised the matter of reverting to Friday as a weekly holiday. The government remained unmoved, but it relented in the matter of showing the 'un-Islamic' contraceptive advertisements on television, moving the already extremely indirect family planning message from prime-time to after ten p.m. During the fasting month of Ramazan, cinemas were asked to drop one show after the opening of the fast.

On 23 December 1999, as if on cue, the Supreme Court Shariat Appellate Bench, deciding an appeal pending with it since 1992, decided to outlaw bank interest as being 'repugnant' to the injunctions of the Koran. It asked the Musharraf government, then busy rescheduling Pakistan's loans with the Paris and London Club creditors, to remove bank interest from loans contracted at home and abroad. This was interpreted by economic experts as a blow delivered by four fundamentalist judges in the higher judiciary to a ruler viewed by them as 'secular'. The clergy welcomed the banning of interest unanimously, followed by the Muslim League whose leader, Nawaz Sharif, was in jail, while the 'independent' press abstained from criticising the judges for fear of arousing reaction among an aggressive clergy.

The government itself did not reject the verdict but took refuge behind a deadline of June 2001 implied in it. Its promise to creditors within and without the country that it would stand by its commitments might not have been credible because of the acceptance by it of the court's deadline. In January 2000, however, Finance Minister Shaukat Aziz categorically pledged the Islamisation of the banking system by June 2001, most probably to put to rest doubts expressed by the Islamists that the government might wriggle out of compliance with the passage of time.

Almost in step with the court's verdict came the incident of the hijacking of an Indian Airlines plane by terrorists who were seen as Pakistanis. India mishandled the hijack and was forced to release a Pakistan-based religious leader said to be the founder of the banned Harkat ul-Ansar. During the hijack drama, India's media let loose an anti-Pakistan barrage which was responded to by Pakistan's state-controlled media and the

*The release of Maulana Masood Azhar was seen by Pakistan
as a victory but it has strengthened the jehadi
elements in the country.*

independent press with equal ferocity. The release by India of
Maulana Masood Azhar was seen by the state in Pakistan as a
victory and a vindication, but it strengthened the fundamentalist jehadi elements in the country, indirectly weakening the
Musharraf government's resolve to take Pakistan towards a
pragmatic approach to the country's problems.

The BJP government's wild accusations against Pakistan
and the Taliban were not credited by the Western media, which
seemed impressed by the behaviour of the two during the hijack
drama. The renamed Harkat ul-Ansar, now called Harkat ul-
Mujahideen, stepped up its fund-raising activity in Punjab
among citizens now convinced of India's 'perfidy after a hijack
it had either botched or engineered to trap Pakistan'. The

fundamentalist-revolutionary clerics, led by the ex-ISI chief, Gen. Hamid Gul, intensified their campaign against the signing of the Comprehensive Test Ban Treaty (CTBT), saying that the army would be disloyal to the country if it acquiesced in it. Any intensification of tensions with India tends to strengthen the fundamentalist elements while the non-fundamentalists indirectly support them by taking part in the anti-India campaign.

Musharraf promised wide-ranging internal reforms after 12 October but ruled out any change in the country's foreign policy. He appointed former foreign secretary Abdul Sattar, known as a hardliner, as foreign minister in his Cabinet, just after the latter had published a response to India's draft nuclear doctrine, recommending that Pakistan test another device to 'upgrade its deterrence' if India went ahead and tested in defiance of the CTBT. However, after a few aggressive statements, Abdul Sattar seemed in December to adopt a low profile in deference to finance minister Shaukat Aziz's effort to create new conditions for the resumption of International Monetary Fund (IMF) assistance and invest-ments at home and from abroad.

Musharraf carefully avoided comment on CTBT, saying that Pakistan would make a decision about signing it after assessing public opinion. In January 2000, Abdul Sattar was shown on TV recommending that Pakistan sign the CTBT 'before India'. A discussion by 'experts' on CTBT in Islamabad later promptly produced a deadlock, and the right-wing press stubbornly defended the earlier decision to sign 'after India'. As for the Afghan policy, Musharraf made certain moves that indicated a 'soft' approach in the wake of the UN Security Council's resolution imposing sanctions on Afghanistan. For Pakistan, the fact that China had not opposed the resolution carried a lot of weight. Pakistani non-Afghan seminarians were prevented from entering Afghanistan to join the Taliban's jehad against the Northern Alliance of Ahmad Shah Massoud. In December 1999, Musharraf paid a very important visit to Teheran and, judging from the opinion expressed by Iran's semi-official press, was given stiff conditions to meet in relation to the Taliban. The Pakistani press carried a report saying that Teheran had offered Pakistan a transit gas pipeline. Later, Musharraf confirmed that Iran had offered to back the project with a billion dollar investment and a pipe rental of six hundred million dollars annually.

On the question of Osama Bin Laden, Musharraf appeared to move Pakistan out of the isolation imposed on it after Saudi Arabia joined the Americans in 1998 to pressure the Taliban government to extradite him. He said he was prepared to discuss the issue. This vague promise signalled his sensitivity to the pro-Osama public opinion in Pakistan, led by the Jamaat's Maulana Fazlur Rehman, who had warned that he would kill all American and European citizens in the country if the government tried to capture Bin Laden. But the government moved quietly against Bin Laden's suspected connections, arresting, according to the press, at least two hundred of his suspected Afghan and Arab agents in December 1999, and elicited from the Americans the statement that they were satisfied by the measures taken by Pakistan in this regard. (The government later denied that it had arrested anyone.)

In 1995, the Pakistani Army had, in a presentation it gave to Michael Krepon of Washington's Stimson Centre, designated

Iran as its strategic retreat area in case of a war with India. But since then, Pakistan has moved solidly behind the Taliban and their anti-Iran war. The Pakistani consensus behind this policy was developed by the army and the ISI beginning 1996 when the Taliban captured Kabul and drove pro-India Ahmad Shah Massoud into the mountains of Panjshir. Pakistan was seen by the international media as the power behind the Taliban's unsuccessful attempt to take the city of Mazar-e-Sharif in Afghanistan in which thousands of Taliban were massacred. In 1998, when the Taliban finally captured Mazar-e-Sharif, they killed and captured a number of Iranian advisers, which plunged the already vitiated Pak-Iran equation into open hostility. The Taliban's siege of Central Afghanistan's Shiite Hazara tribes, and their rough behaviour with the international NGOs in Kabul, brought further negative fallout. Pakistan's bottom-line was its India-driven policy which saw Iran and India arrayed behind the Northern Alliance.

The year 1999 saw Pakistan increasingly isolated on Afghanistan as the Americans and the Russians moved behind the international consensus against the Taliban. Ahmad Shah Massoud embarrassed Pakistan further by revealing that he had hundreds of Pakistani prisoners of war in his custody, including seventeen officers of the Pakistani Army which, according to one report published in the Pakistani press, were disowned by Pakistan 'because they were all retired from service and could have gone to Afghanistan on their own.'

In Pakistan, the Afghan policy has often been considered as one with few or no options, particularly because the Kandahar government of Mullah Umar was not always amenable to 'advice' from Islamabad. The Taliban are all Pakhtun linked by their ethnicity and Deobandi faith to the majority Pakhtuns living in the NWFP and Balochistan. The rapid spread of the Deobandi militias and seminaries in Punjab during the Afghan jehad against the Soviets, and the utilisation of Deobandi militias in Kashmir as a low-cost option, has made it even more difficult to effect changes in an increasingly untenable Afghan policy. Pakistan has had to sacrifice a great deal internally since the 1980s when it began its Saudi and American-funded jehad in Afghanistan.

In 1986, General Zia allowed the Afghan mujahideen to attack the Shiite Turi tribe in the Kurram Agency of its Tribal Areas abutting Afghanistan, and a large number of Turis suspected of non-cooperation with the mujahideen and of having an alliance with the government in Kabul were killed. In response to this action, a Shiite party, Tehreek-e-Nifaz-e-Fiqh-e-Jaafaria, was created with a Turi cleric, Ariful Hussaini, as its chief. Hussaini was murdered in Peshawar in 1989, which the Shiite community thought was the handiwork of General Zia, who was in turn killed in an air crash within a fortnight of the assassination. This began a series of killings of Shiite Pakistanis and Iranian diplomats and officials in Pakistan. The Deobandi parties, especially Sipah-e-Sihaba, spread their influence to the Northern Areas where the Shiites and the Ismailis were made to submit to their puritanical aggression.

The rise of the sectarian sentiment in Pakistan, and the increased support of the Pakistani Army to the anti-Shiite Taliban, stiffened the Afghan policy and subliminally made it a policy of national consensus. As the year 2000 began, General Musharraf was hard put to make changes in it now probably demanded by his own advisers. In any case, the Afghan policy remains marginally more flexible than the policy on Kashmir. The fact that India is not willing to discuss Kashmir with Pakistan has removed for the time being the pressure to change it in light of the pro-India international opinion.

The civil war in Afghanistan and the jehad in Kashmir have gradually replaced the modernist-Islamic mujahideen fighters with more conservative ones: the Jamaat-e-Islami consensus among the Pakhtun fighters has veered to a Deobandi consensus. The dominant Hizb-e-Islami of Gulbuddin Hekmatyar, a flag-bearer of modernist-Islamist thinking, lost favour with the Pakistani establishment. In its place, the Taliban of Mullah Umar, trained in the traditional

*The civil war in Afghanistan and the jehad in Kashmir have replaced modernist-Islamist thinking with a more conservative, Deobandi consensus.*

Deobandi jurisprudence, enjoy growing popularity in Pakistan. In Kashmir, Jamaat-e-Islami's Hizbul Mujahideen has been eclipsed by Harkat ul-Ansar (now Harkat ul-Mujahideen after being declared a terrorist organisation by Washington) of Deobandi persuasion.

In a parallel development, the Wahabi or Ahle Hadis warriors have gained strength. The most effective jehadi outfit based in Lahore is Lashkar-e-Toeba, functioning as a subordinate branch of Dawat al-Irshad, an organisation with contacts in the Arab world which collects jehad funds from the expatriate Muslim communities in the West. The Lashkar has training camps in Afghanistan and 'Azaad' Kashmir and is arguably the most resourceful militia fighting in Kashmir. In Afghanistan, Osama Bin Laden has strengthened the old Wahabi connection with the Deobandi Taliban rulers. Some American sources claim that the Taliban Amirul Momineen, Mullah Umar, has married Bin Laden's daughter.

The third strand of the fundamentalist movement which joins the Wahabi-Deobandi combine in Afghanistan is the Naqshbandiya from Central Asia. Uzbek Islamist leaders Juma Namangani and Tahir Yuldashev have staged a fundamentalist revolt against Uzbekistan's president Karimov and have sought shelter with the Taliban government after being accused by Karimov of trying to assassinate him in Tashkent. In Afghanistan, the naqshbandiya faith was already strongly represented by Sibghatullah Mujadiddi, Afghanistan's first president chosen by the mujahideen in Peshawar in 1989. Mujadiddi is in direct line of descent from Sheikh Ahmad of Sirhind, also called Mujaddid Alfe Sani, who led a mystical movement of purification under Emperor Jehangir and was greatly admired by Islamic revivalist movements in India.

All three movements, the Deobandi, the Ahle Hadis-Wahabi, and Naqshbandi, are against bidaa (innovation) in Islamic rituals. They opposed the eclecticism that developed among Muslims under the Mughals and wished to separate local accretions from the pure Islamic faith. The founder of the Naqshbandiya order compelled the Mughal king Jehangir to persecute the Sikhs and the Muslim mystical orders which had developed a spiritual consensus with the Hindus. The other preoccupation of the Naqshbandiya in India was opposition to the Shiite faith developing in the south of India and in the northern province of Oudh. Shaikh Ahmad had decreed that the Shiites were apostates and had to be put to the sword.

*When Leghari (seen here with Narasimha Rao) was sacked as president by Nawaz Sharif he paid secret visits to the Chakwal madrassa in affirmation of his close contacts with the army.*

In Pakistan, only one naqshbandi militant religious outfit called Tanzeem al-Ikhwan is active under the aggressive leadership of Maulana Akram Awan. Based on the mystical teachings of Shaikh Ahmad, the madrassa run by him in Chakwal has close links with the army. Farooq Ahmad Khan Leghari, after his ouster from presidentship by Nawaz Sharif, paid secret visits to the seminary in Chakwal in affirmation of his close contacts with the Pakistani Army. In the investigations that followed the 1995 unsuccessful military coup in Pakistan, led by Islamist officers, Maulana Akram Awan's name had cropped up in the list of the accused but was removed from the findings because of his close army connections. This gives evidence of the militarisation of the Central Asia mystical order.

The Pakhtun population of Balochistan is entirely Deobandi and traditionally anti-Shiite. The Pakistan army chief after Ayub Khan, Gen. Musa Khan, a Shiite Hazara, had himself buried in Iran through his will because of the Deobandi dominance in his province. In his book, *Unholy Wars: Afghanistan, America and International Terrorism*, John K. Cooley reveals that Mullah Umar and Osama Bin Laden first met in 1989 in a Deobandi mosque, Masjid Binuri, in Karachi, and, under the tutelage of Pakistan's most powerful cleric, Mufti Nizamuddin Shamzai, presumably formed an alliance based on the traditional closeness of the Deobandis, who follow the Hanafi school, with the Wahabis, who accept only hadith under Abdul Wahab. Thus the protection offered to Bin Laden by the Taliban, and the threats delivered by Pakistan's Jamaat leaders to American citizens in support of Bin Laden, seem to spring from an historical interface between the two schools of Islamic fiqh (jurisprudence).

The non-Pakhtun population of Pakistan is predominantly

Barelvi, following the Hanafi fiqh of Ahmad Raza Khan Barelvi (1856-1931) who led a successful revolt in India against the stringent teachings of the Deobandi-Wahabi school of thought. The stronghold of Barelvism remains Punjab, the largest province of Pakistan in terms of population, but increasingly the state-controlled mosques are being given to Deobandi khateebs (sermon-readers). Because of the rise of the Deobandi militias, and their funding by the Arabs for their anti-Shiite and anti-Iran doctrine, the province is rapidly losing its Barelvi temperament. The Tablighi Jamaat which holds its annual congregation in Lahore has become a powerful influence favouring a Deobandi point of view. It gathers two million people in its annual congregation but it is important to note that over ninety per cent of its attendants are Pakhtun from Peshawar and the Tribal Areas bordering Afghanistan. The Pakistan president, Muhammad Rafiq Tarar, is a Punjabi Deobandi.

The Afghan war pushed over three million Afghan refugees into Pakistan, which accommodated them in the Pakhtun-dominated areas of the NWFP and Balochistan. The Afghan youth, trained in the Deobandi seminaries in these two provinces for over ten years, later became the Taliban warriors of Mullah Umar. In their war with the Northern Alliance, the Taliban armies are constantly 'replenished' by fresh Taliban from Pakistan, many of them now Punjabi. According to Ahmed Rashid in *Foreign Affairs* (November-December 1999), over 80,000 Taliban have gone to Afghanistan to fight the Deobandi war against the Northern Alliance of Ahmad Shah Massoud. Recognition of the Taliban government by Saudi Arabia and Pakistan can be seen also in light of the 'confluence' of historically anti-Shiite Deobandi-Wahabi spiritual coalition.

This has pitted a Shiite Iran against them. After the Naqshbandi addition to this equation, the Central Asian states too have joined the anti-Taliban reaction, with Russia at their back, and America inclining in favour of this formation because of Osama Bin Laden.

The fear of 'Talibanisation' in Pakistan springs from the circumstantial evidence of 'stiffening' in its ideology. Most of the 26,000 religious seminaries have undergone a sea change. For instance, in the case of the Barelvi organisation, Dawat-e-Islami, which holds an impressive 200,000-strong congregation in Multan in Punjab annually, the prohibition of human image is a change in the direction of Wahabi-Deobandi opposition to television and photographs. In their *obiter dicta*, the judges of the lower and higher judiciary have inclined to a more fundamentalist view of Islam. The lower courts have been handing out death sentences to non-Muslims (including Ahmedis who were forcibly declared non-Muslims in 1974) under the Draconian Gustakh-e-Rasul or blasphemy law. Christians have been particularly targeted by Muslim clergy in the rural areas often led by the jehadi militias. In 1997, a Christian settlement in Punjab, Shantinagar, was razed to the ground by militias using incendiary bombs normally a part of the arsenal of the mujahideen in Kashmir. In 1998, Bishop John Joseph of Faisalabad, Punjab, committed suicide in front of a court trying a Christian for blasphemy, and unleashed reaction from the European Union and the US, the latter passing a law mandating sanctions against states relying on blasphemy to violate human rights.

In Lahore, the high court handed down a verdict in 1996

against girls marrying without the permission of their fathers; it went against the Hanafi jurisprudence in force in Pakistan. Before the verdict was struck down by the Supreme Court of Pakistan, a controversy developed on the issue in which the clerics generally upheld the more stringent Wahabi law applied by the high court.

Encouraged by the growing conservative outlook in the judiciary, Islamist scholars went to court in 1998 to undo some of the reforms initiated in 1961 in respect of Muslim Family Law. Petitioners, including some professors teaching Islamic courses in the universities, asked the court to strike down the provision of registering the *nikah* (marriage deed) with the local councils and remove the limit placed on the marriageable age of girls.

The Supreme Court began hearing a 1992 government appeal against an old Shariat court verdict that bank interest be abolished in Pakistan. The Nawaz Sharif government, already having tabled its own 15th Amendment Shariat Bill under pressure from the fundamentalist forces in society, indicated its willingness to accept the ban on bank interest. The Supreme Court, judging from the highly publicised remarks of the judges in the course of hearings, was about to deliver a verdict against bank interest or riba before the 12 October coup took place. It shocked most Pakistanis when it finally delivered its verdict against bank interest on 23 December, knowing full well that it would create insurmountable difficulties for the Musharraf government. The judge who headed the Supreme Court bench had headed the Lahore high court when it handed down the verdict that women could not marry without the permission of their fathers. Encouraged by all this, the Council of Islamic Ideology declared that jails were against Islam and should be abolished. Leaders of the Deobandi parties have been calling for the introduction of a stringent Taliban-like system in Pakistan. On a trip to the Frontier Province in 1998, Prime Minister Nawaz Sharif actually promised the enforcement of such a system, which he later denied.

T he Talibanisation of the state dates back to the days when Pakistan began handling the Afghan jehad against the Soviets. That the army was the first party affected by this process is proved by the reverse indoctrination experienced by the officers of the Inter Services Intelligence (ISI). At least two former heads of ISI, Gen. Hamid Gul and Gen. Javed Nasir, today stand at the head of the Islamic movement in Pakistan and enjoy leverage over governments by reason of their contacts with the militias on the one hand and the army on the other. Both favour an Islamic revolution which will wean Pakistan away from its perceived cultural and political alignment with the West in general and the US in particular. They represent also the intense anti-Indian orientation of the army and the common people.

Of the two, General Gul is the more outspoken. His most recent sally against Musharraf was delivered after the government was seen to trim its political sails to become eligible for fresh assistance from the IMF and rescheduling of old loans with the London and Paris clubs of creditors. He warned in a newspaper statement that 'this government too' was treading the old pro-American path and was preparing to sign the CTBT and 'embrace Vajpayee'. Another former ISI chief, General Durrani, although inclined to be secular in outlook, writes often to consolidate the old foreign policy paradigm favoured in the past by the armed forces. It is noteworthy that General Gul, General Durrani as well as Gen. Javed Nasir were removed as ISI chiefs under the shadow of suspicion. At the time of writing, the last chief of the ISI, General Ziauddin, along with two other former ISI officers, were in custody and may be subjected to court martial for anti-state activities.

The return to Pakistan of Maulana Masood Azhar after his release from India following the deal made with the hijackers in Kandahar brought to the fore the importance of the Binuri Masjid seminary in Karachi as Asia's biggest centre of Deobandi-Taliban power. Maulana Azhar headed for Karachi after entering Pakistan and embarrassed Islamabad by making his usual anti-India and anti-US speeches at the mosque in Binuri Town. Washington, which was to judge whether India was correct in accusing Pakistan of being a terrorist state, lodged a strong protest against his outpourings.

The chief of the Binuri Town madrassa is Mufti Nizamuddin Shamzai, a Pakhtun Deobandi cleric who counts Afghanistan's Mulla Umar among his disciples. He is said to be the most powerful man in Pakistan — he sits at the top of the Deobandi consensus — and is the author of a fatwa of death against Americans. After the Kandahar hijacking, jehad funds were collected all over Pakistan in his name. In Lahore, for instance, the Masjid-e-Shuhada, a government-controlled mosque given under a Deobandi khateeb (sermon-reader), collected donations under banners carrying the Mufti's name as guarantor. The Binuri mosque madrassa was set up in 1947 by another Pakhtun cleric, Mufti Yusuf Binuri, who had inherited the 'militant' branch of Deoband's Dar al-Ulum, while

Peshawar remained the centre of the 'monastic' branch headed by Mufti Mahmood, father of the present Jamaat chief, Maulana Fazlur Rehman.

The Deobandi cleric who led the funeral prayer of Jinnah in 1948 in Karachi, Maulana Shabbir Ahmad Usmani, was also in the 'monastic' tradition, but some saw irony in the fact that a Shia-hating cleric performed the last rites of a leader whom his sister, Fatima Jinnah, was to declare Shiite in an affidavit to the Sindh high court a few days later. The fear of Talibanisation spread in Pakistan in 1997 after the Binuri-Taliban seminarians virtually took over the city of Karachi for a day during a protest. It was realised for the first time that the Taliban power was now centred in Karachi, heretofore seen as a business city with a 'secular' character, and not in the NWFP and Balochistan.

The biggest persuader in Pakistan is the economy. It can't be imagined how the military rulers can blackball suggestions coming from their civilian Cabinet to re-align Pakistan's foreign policy behind a global consensus for peace in the region. India may be in a better position to defy this consensus because of its good economic indicators and the international goodwill it has reaped from the Kargil operation, but Pakistan has no options left. Musharraf and his colleagues may be struggling with the single-option direction being dictated by the country's economy, but will most probably adjust to it as time passes, unless, of course, there is an interruption of rule.

Musharraf's replacement can come in two ways. Finding the going too tough, Musharraf can curtail his rule and hold elections, or he can be replaced through a 'revolution' against his perceived 'secular' and pro-American posture. In the first instance, the new elected government will quickly fall into the old groove of a cautious approach to regional and world affairs without the ability to make the radical changes to stem Pakistan's economic retrogression. It will not be able to ignore the agenda of the Pakistani Army to keep the Kashmir pot boiling, nor will it be equal to the task of taking Pakistan out of international isolation in Afghanistan. Fundamentalism in Pakistan will intensify and challenge the elected government on such measures as the complete Islamisation of society and the national economy. The Pakistani public, already disenchanted with politicians, will incline more and more in favour of the clergy and thus render the state vulnerable to a take-over by Islamists through a 'revolution'.

The second mode of possible transition is a coup by another general on behalf of the Islamists. Fundamentalism in Pakistan is kept at bay by democracy: the electorate repeatedly votes in favour of the 'secular' parties, leaving the religious parties marginalised in parliament. For this reason, most religious leaders have been talking of 'revolution' instead of victory through elections. The 'revolution', if it happens, will bring the Sunni clergy to power, which will somehow have to paper over their doctrinal differences to be able to rule. The fundamentalist government will immediately adopt an aggressive posture towards India in particular and the US and the West in general, seeing a Jewish-Hindu collusion in their attitude towards Pakistan.

A fundamentalist regime will also turn on the economy with a determination to impose statist reforms, nationalising and centralising a number of sectors in order to realise the ideal of Islamic falahi (welfare) state. An economic collapse is sure to follow this policy since Pakistan does not enjoy the isolationist cushion of Iran's oil wealth, and disorder will envelop the country, including a civil war-like situation in Sindh and Balochistan. It is this fear that compels most secularists in Pakistan to see Musharraf's government as Pakistan's last defence against its Talibanisation.

# Who Owns Pakistan?

## SHAHID-UR-REHMAN

The *Kyodo News* correspondent in Pakistan on how four interest groups — the military, the civil service, the feudal lords and the industrial barons — have ruled the country.

In the 1960s, Pakistan was regarded by some as a country on its way to becoming the first Asian tiger. Delegations from South Korea and Indonesia visited Pakistan to study its models for economic development and population control. However, as we enter the new millennium, Pakistan is being described as a failed state, a country in the process of a meltdown, its economy being kept afloat by the International Monetary Fund (IMF) and the World Bank. The latest to join this chorus is Dr Hafeez Pasha, twice deputy chairman, Planning Commission and presently chairman of the macroeconomic group of the military government of Gen. Pervez Musharraf, who believes that Pakistan needs 'an economic survival plan,' not an economic revival plan.

Musharraf has set for himself an ambitious agenda that amounts to rewriting the Constitution and reinventing democracy. But will he succeed in giving even a semblance of democracy and stability to Pakistan, let alone real stability and real democracy? Will he triumph over the heavy economic and administrative odds confronting his government, the heaviest of which is corruption?

It seems to be an impossible mission. Consider, for example, the catalogue of problems that Musharraf faces on the economic front alone: Pakistan today has a foreign debt of thirty-five billion dollars; its exports have stagnated at eight billion dollars; and three of its main industries — textiles, cement and sugar manufacturing — are bogged down in chronic structural problems. The likely fate of his government's bid to revive economic activity is evident from the fact that the don of Pakistani industrialists, Nasim Saigol, Pakistan's equivalent of Tata and Birla, and his nephew are in jail, and foreign investors are on the run because of a running dispute with independent power producers. The privatisation process on which every government since 1988 has pinned its hopes to generate some revenues has run afoul (eighty industrial units, financial institutions and utilities had been privatised amid stories of rampant corruption, and the present government has announced a complete review of the strategy of privatisation). The government's tax net is designed to catch small fish but has holes through which crocodiles can swim through, its utilities are breaking down, and financial institutions are bogged down in the quagmire of bad debts which account for nearly one-third of its banking assets.

The enormity and complexity of the task that has been entrusted by Musharraf to his banker finance minister Shaukat Aziz can also be gauged from the experience of Shahid Javed Burki, who quit his job with the World Bank in Washington to become finance minister in the caretaker government of Malik Meraj Khalid in 1996. Burki was the embodiment of confidence when he declared at an airport press conference on his arrival from Washington that 'I have been preparing for this job since I was ten years old.' Three months later, when he was leaving the government, he told me he was returning to Washington a depressed man because he never realised the enormity of Pakistan's economic problems, the biggest of which was corruption.

Burki and others like him have failed because though Pakistan was designed to be a welfare state, it has grown into an elitist one and it is in the interest of the ruling elite to maintain the status quo. Those assigned the task of fixing the economy skirted around the real solution because it would have meant committing hara-kiri, or at least dropping a heavy stone on their own feet. The result: Pakistan today resembles the proverbial patient asking the doctor to 'first heal thyself.'

Pakistan is a joint venture of four nationalities but has been ruled, except for a brief period of Zulfiqar Ali Bhutto (December 1971-July 1976), in regular turns by four interest groups or their coalition. The four ethnic nationalities that constitute a population of 130 million people are the Punjabis, the Sindhis, the Pathans and the Baluchis. (Pakistan is not a nation. It is a crowd brought together by an accident of history, Pathan leader Wali Khan has often said.) But the four groups that have ruled Pakistan alternately, as if allocated their turn in an invisible game of musical chairs, are the military, the bureaucracy, the feudal lords and the industrial barons. Making up the nucleus of these four interest groups are twelve corps commanders, nearly two thousand landowners owning more than half of the cultivable land, a cadre of nearly one thousand officers of District Management Group (DMG) and Police Service of Pakistan (PSP), and forty-four industrial families.

To take the bureaucracy first, the Pakistan government employs 2.9 million people at a cost of eighty-two billion rupees per annum and according to a World Bank study, this is not a large number by international standards. However, the study misses the point that between 1990 and 1997 the real growth in bureaucracy has taken place among the employees of grade 16-22, who have a high incidence of corruption because of the decision- and policy-making power vested in them. The number of lower-grade employees has remained almost static.

The District Management Group and the Police Service of Pakistan are known as the most powerful, and customs and excise as the most corrupt of the civil services. The DMG and PSP currently have a cadre of nearly eight hundred members who form the pillar of the administrative structure in Pakistan.

It is about the bureaucrats of this class that an article in *Dawn* newspaper recently said: 'Never before in our history has it (the bureaucracy) played so negative a role ... it must be kept in mind that the bureaucracy will overtly and covertly resist devolution because it perceives this as a threat to its own power base.'

The basic administrative unit in Pakistan is the patwari — there are 9,500 of them all over the country. The power of the patwari is legendary — according to one popular anecdote, an aged woman receiving help from the president of Pakistan at a function prayed to god to elevate him to the office of the patwari! The patwaris maintain the records of ownership, sale and transfer of land and of area cultivated for different crops, etc. For several years, the government has been trying to computerise their records but the move is being resisted since a big chunk of land is owned in fictitious names. The patwaris are the main collaborators with the big landlords who continue to hold tens of thousands of acres of land, in violation of the land reforms that restrict individual ownership to 150 acres. These landowners register their lands in the names of wives, children, and fictitious identity cards.

The commissioner is the head of the highest administrative unit, i.e a division. Emma Duncan, in her book *Breaking the Curfew*, observed that these commissioners, living in palace-like houses, have seats reserved on each PIA flight leaving the airport in their jurisdiction.

The interest group which has provided the majority of prime ministers and parliamentarians in Pakistan is that of agricultural landlords. Pakistan has 3.5 million landowners. About two thousand of them own seventy per cent of cultivable land, protecting their estates with private armies and controlling the lives of tens of millions of people who work as tenant farmers and sharecroppers. In the national assembly they are represented by the Daultanas, the Timmans, the Jatois, the Bhuttos, the Legharis and the Khurros. It is believed that four out of five seats in the national assembly are occupied by these people, their offspring or relatives.

Wadera Ghulam Mohammad Mehr, who died in 1995, owned a hundred thousand acres of land, a fact that was confirmed to me by his Oxford-educated grandson at their ancestral home in Khan Pur Sharif, which is a one-and-a-half-hour drive from the main Grand Trunk Road. I asked the junior Mehr if it was true that land from the GT Road right upto Khan Pur Sharif belonged to their family.

'And from here to the Indian border also,' (which was perhaps another hour's drive), was the proud reply.

In 1990 when the Benazir Bhutto government was sacked, Ghulam Mustafa Jatoi was appointed the caretaker prime minister. A former Indian ambassador to Pakistan, S.K. Singh, wrote in a newspaper article that Jatoi was Pakistan's biggest landlord, owning eighty thousand acres of land. During a visit to India, I had the chance to ask Singh how he knew that Jatoi owned eighty thousand acres. 'Jatoi himself told me,' was the reply.

Nawaz Sharif's family alone is known to own four thousand acres of land at Raiwind on the outskirts of Lahore. Sharif has built four palatial houses on the land for himself, his two brothers and his parents. The estate is called Amar Jati, after Sharif's ancestral village in Amritsar. Sharif's cousins and uncles own another four thousand acres in the same vicinity.

*A worker cuts grass outside Sharif's home on Raiwind Estate — spread over 4000 acres — near Lahore. Sharif has four palatial houses on the estate for himself and his family.*

Benazir Bhutto has often alleged that former President Farooq Leghari used his influence to take back large tracts of land that was expropriated in the land reforms carried out by Zulfiqar Ali Bhutto in 1972. The same had happened with the earlier land reforms by Ayub Khan when 2.35 million acres of land was recovered from big landlords but at least 4.5 lakh acres was handed back to them for maintenance of orchards and Shikargahs (farm ranges).

The concentration of wealth in the hands of a rich industrial class — nicknamed 'Twenty-two families' in 1968 by the then government's chief economist, Dr Mahboob-ul-Haq — contributed in the rapid fermentation of the seeds of discontent, culminating in the emergence of Bangladesh in 1971. Dr Haq had pointed out that Pakistan's economy had come to be dominated by twenty-two families who owned sixty-six per cent of the total industrial assets, seventy per cent of insurance and eighty per cent of banking. These families were dominated by four immigrant, business communities from India — the Memons, the Khojas, the Bohras and the Ismaelis — and the Chiniotis from Pakistani Punjab but included no native Bengali, Sindhi or Baluchi. The Memons were the most powerful of the lot.

Soviet scholar Sergi Levin, in his article, 'The Memons of Pakistan,' published in 1975, estimated that every fourth company in the 1960s belonged to a Memon family. Lawrence White, an American scholar who studied the concentration of wealth during the same period, found thirteen Memons among the top forty-two industrial families in Pakistan. These included Kassim Dada, whose ancestors had set up the well-known firm of Dada Abdullah and Company which sent M.K. Gandhi to South Africa as their legal representative in 1890.

The separation of East Pakistan brought the socialist government of Zulfiqar Ali Bhutto to power and his whirlwind nationalisation of key industries, banks and insurance became a turning point in Pakistan's politics and economy. It broke the back of several leading business houses. Those who escaped nationalisation were broken in spirit and moved abroad, thus triggering an outflow of capital and capitalists. There was also a perpetual confrontation between native Sindhis (sons of the soil) and Mohajirs (migrants from India) during the 1971-86 period under Z.A. Bhutto and Zia ul-Haq. The exodus was particularly heavy from Karachi as most industrialists there were Mohajirs. Several leading Karachi industrialists, including

Ahmad Dawood, Fancy, Haroon and Rangoonwala, left Pakistan for good, some of them returning only in their old age.

The exodus of the Karachi-based business groups, particularly the Memons, known as 'the sailor business-men from India,' became a windfall for the small business groups of the Chiniotis from Punjab. The Chiniotis, who hailed from Chiniot in southwestern Punjab, had migrated to Calcutta, Kanpur and Madras in the early twentieth century and set themselves up in the trade of leather, hides and skins. After Partition, these businessmen returned to Pakistan and started trading in food grains, rice, cotton, textiles and other commodities. Some of the Chiniotis — represented by firms such as Colony, Crescent and Nishat — had joined the twenty-two

*Under Zia and later under Nawaz Sharif, government facilities came to be monopolised by a handful of industrialists from Punjab, also called the Lahore mafia.*

families by 1970 but a whole lot of them catapulted to the top in Pakistan's corporate sector under Zia ul-Haq and later Nawaz Sharif. Until Zia took over, there were few industrialists from Punjab. But under Zia and later under Nawaz Sharif, credit, licensing, raw material and other government facilities came to be monopolised by a handful of industrialists from Punjab. This group came to be known as the Lahore mafia and was dominated by Chinioti businessmen.

Sindh was the home province of Bhutto whom Zia had hanged in 1979 on charges of a political murder, and it became a bastion of agitation against his military government. It is said that the Mohajir Qaumi Movement (MQM) owes its existence to the quest by Zia to create a counter-force to the Pakistan People's Party in Sindh. There was eyeball-to-eyeball confrontation between the Sindhis and Mohajirs. Kidnapping for ransom, and attacks on pockets of rival population became the order of the day.

The situation triggered another flight of capital and capitalists from Sindh to Europe, the US and the Middle East. Others with roots and relatives in Punjab migrated to tax-free industrial estates that were cropping up in that state under an industrialist chief minister Nawaz Sharif.

'The Memons are finished in Pakistan. They have been wiped out deliberately,' maintained Yusuf Haroon, the top Memon industrialist and first chief minister of Sindh after independence, in an interview with me in 1997. Once ranked among the top twenty-two industrialists, Haroon has wound up his business in Pakistan and now lives in New York in an apartment overlooking the Central Park.

Haroon was bitter with the Punjabi politicians and rulers starting with the Nawab of Kalabagh under Ayub Khan to Zia and Nawaz Sharif. He believed that the seeds of discontent against the federation of Pakistan were planted in smaller provinces with the shifting of the capital to Islamabad. He claimed that immediately after Pakistan was born and he was appointed chief minister of Sindh, the Quaid-e-Azam had asked him to look for a site to shift the capital from Karachi. The first prime minister, Liaquat Ali Khan, visited and favoured a site proposed by him in Balochistan, about two hundred kilometres from Karachi on the Arabian coast. But the site was rejected because President Ayub Khan, a military-general from northern Pakistan, and his right hand man, Nawaz Amir Khan of Kalabagh, who was governor of West Pakistan, wanted the capital in Punjab, at the place which is now called Islamabad.

Nawaz Sharif was a reaction to Zulfiqar Ali Bhutto and he tried to reincarnate the twenty-two families through the privatisation of government industries and corporations and through other government policies. Under his privatisation plans, government-owned corporations, banks, utilities, roads, airports, railways, bridges, government rest houses and prime estate land were to come under the hammer. If his plans had materialised, he would have gone down in Pakistan's history as a modern-day King Richard, who had declared, 'I would sell London, if I find a suitable buyer.' His three-year rule created such grotesque inequalities that Dr Mahboob-ul-Haq saw Pakistan becoming a banana republic or a Latin American state.

According to a study completed in 1997, forty-four industrial groups owned manufacturing and financial assets worth five hundred billion rupees, which was equal to Pakistan's annual budget. Of these twenty-two had their roots in Punjab, of which fifteen belonged to Chiniotis.

The Punjab-based groups accounted for total assets of Rs 342 billion, Rs 107 billion in manufacturing assets and Rs 235 billion in financial assets. These groups owned 212 of 552 non-financial companies listed on the stock exchange, accounting for forty-three per cent of the manufacturing assets. Out of 175 financial, investment and leasing companies listed in Pakistan, seventy-six belonged to these groups. Seven of the top ten groups — Nishat, Saigol, Crescent, Ittefaq, Chakwal, Saphire-Gulistan and Packages — hailed from Punjab, against four in 1970.

Pakistan today is in a social, political and administrative mess. It is at war with itself — there is a war among the four 'nationalities', between Shiites and Sunnis, between the provinces and the federation, between the rulers and the ruled.

Pinning top priority to revive economic activity, Musharraf has appointed a Pakistani banker of international repute with Citibank, Shaukat Aziz, as his finance minister and inducted several leading businessmen in the federal and provincial cabinets. Razak Dawood, scion of a leading Memon family, has been appointed federal minister for industries and commerce; Abbas Sarfraz, another leading businessman from North West Frontier Province (NWFP), has been inducted as minister for Kashmir affairs. Salim Altaf, member of the Crescent group, is the new chairman of the privatisation commission. The head of another leading industrial group, Dewan, has been included as minister of industries in the provincial government of Sindh.

Will Musharraf succeed in rebuilding national confidence

and morale, restoring national cohesion and reviving economic activity? Well, one need only point out that the two key political players in Sindh, Benazir Bhutto and Altaf Hussain, are in exile and Nawaz Sharif, whose power base in Punjab can hardly be questioned, is languishing in prison.

A story that the late Dr Mahboob-ul-Haq often narrated about a brain-storming session with a group of over hundred Pakistani students in a hotel in Boston tells of the difficulties faced by any ruler trying to forge national cohesion in Pakistan. Dr Haq said that at the end of his session, lasting several hours, he asked the students as to how many of them were planning to return to Pakistan after completing their studies. Only three students raised their hands. Those who were staying back said they were sure they would get very goods jobs in the US because they were at the top in the subjects of their study. However, they were not sure if they would find appropriate jobs back in Pakistan where the quota system was in operation and sifarish (recommendation) or closeness to a politician and not merit was the prerequisite for any decent job.

The quota system was originally envisaged in Pakistan's Constitution for fifteen years to help allow the underdeveloped regions to catch up with the developed ones. But it has continued now for thirty years and has been exploited by the rich and the powerful (politicians and the civil and military bureaucracy) to induct their wards into the ruling clique, at the cost of merit and efficiency. Thus, native Sindhis and Mohajirs are alienated from the political mainstream as students from rural Sindh get preference over them in admissions to professional colleges and jobs.

According to the results of the latest superior services held by the Public Service Commission, out of 217 vacancies available in 1999 only twenty-three were to be filled on merit and the rest on quota. The quota for Punjab was 108, Sindh (rural) twenty-four, Sindh (urban) nineteen, NWFP twenty-five, Balochistan four, Tribal Area nine and Azad Kashmir five.

Corruption in Pakistan has created legends. It was ranked as the second most corrupt country in the world under the first Benazir Bhutto government. It is estimated that ten per cent of the government budget of five hundred billion rupees is lost in 'transmission,' the word used for embezzlement in Islamabad's bureaucratic jargon. Nationalised commercial banks sanctioned credits worth nearly Rs 406 billion last year for which the going commission rate was ten per cent. While ten per cent has been the standard measure of graft and transmission losses in most government departments, the Central Board of Revenue, Pakistan's equivalent of the Indian Revenue Service, has the reputation of being the most corrupt organisation in Pakistan. Its revenue estimates are projected at Rs 350 billion and industry estimates are that an equal amount goes to line the pockets of the twenty thousand revenue collectors.

Smuggling of goods through Afghanistan, India, Iran and China is estimated at three billion dollars (Rs 150 billion). The smuggled goods include cloth, betel leaves, whisky, pharmaceutical products and consumer goods from India; carpets, plastic, cheap garments, petrol and petroleum products from Iran; and electronics and consumer goods from Afghanistan. During recent years, Chinese goods have also been coming in via the checkpost at Sust bordering Xinjiang province.

A study by United Narcotics Drug Control Agency

provisionally placed the income from narcotics smuggling at 1.5 billion dollars (Rs 75 billion) per annum. Most of this drug money goes to several families in Pakistan's tribal belt, particularly the Afridis and the Kukekhels. The customs officials too have a big stake in the drug trade.

The twenty-six persons arrested or charged with corruption and bank loan default on 17 October 1999 by the present rulers represent the elite who have ruled Pakistan since 1986, the year of Pakistan's return to managed democracy. Apart from Nawaz Sharif, these include Benazir and her husband Asif Zardari; Jaffer Leghari and Anwar Saifullah, brother and son-in-law respectively of two former presidents; a former navy chief and a former air force chief, and several parliamentarians.

One of the twenty-six names, that of Mian Aftab, deserves special mention to give an idea of the way Pakistani banks have been systematically robbed. Mian Aftab's group, Fazal Sons, is among the forty-four top groups in Pakistan and he was one of the three brothers who inherited Cotton Textile Mills and a few other small units from his father. He found out that borrowing money in collusion with bankers was far more remunerative than setting up industrial units. In 1993 when Moeen Qureshi published the list of loan defaulters, his Fazal Sons group was defaulting in payment of thirty-four loans to all the nationalised banks. The publication of the list forced him to flee. He is currently living in Europe, operating a chain of three hotels and a health club in the UK. Habib Bank has moved a court in the UK to freeze his assets and the Pakistan government has asked Interpol to bring him back to Pakistan.

A paper read out at the annual conference of Pakistan Institute of Development Economics (PIDE) in Islamabad estimated on the basis of variation between the international trade figures and Pakistan government data that Pakistani industrialists and traders have stashed away nearly fifty billion dollars of foreign exchange earnings abroad.

In 1996, when the Benazir Bhutto government was sacked for the second time, the charge sheet included addresses of villas owned by Asif Zardari and his father Hakim Ali Zardari in France and at least another European location. Benazir Bhutto is accused of owning a three million pound sterling estate in Surrey while Nawaz Sharif and his family have three posh villas in London. Several leading Pakistani businessmen have shifted their businesses to Jabal-e-Ali near Dubai and several leading politicians and businessmen are known to be operating hotels in the Far East, the Middle East, Europe and at Florida and Houston in the US.

Since 1988, every government has faithfully negotiated a new package with the IMF and depended heavily on foreign capital inflow and official aid. While talking of hard decisions they resorted to resource mobilisation by taxing the common man through a reckless increase in the prices of utilities and petroleum products. That is exactly what seems to be the desire of Musharraf and his banker finance minister.

Nawaz Sharif rode into power in 1996 after an election campaign in which he championed the 'breaking of the begging bowl.' However, in December 1998, when he travelled to the US on an official visit and held talks with the IMF and World Bank, the BBC commented in one of its reports that no Third World leader had ever come to Washington to beg so royally.

On 15 December 1999, Musharraf's government announced a ten per cent increase in the price of petroleum products. In his televised address to the nation that followed two days later, Musharraf observed that the economy was in a state far worse than initially assessed after the 12 October coup. He announced the imposition of a general sales tax on retail trade and directed the relevant officials to present him a report within one month about the situation with regard to parleys with independent power producers. There was a chorus of condemnation from the political and business quarters that the new package was nothing but the policy framework envisaged by an agreement with the IMF and World Bank and which was on hold since Pakistan carried out nuclear tests in May 1998.

Before its ouster, the Nawaz Sharif government had hammered out an arrangement with the IMF, the World Bank, the Asian Development Bank and donor countries for rescheduling 3.9 billion dollars of foreign debt, envisaging separate agreements with individual creditors. The finalisation of some of these came to the lot of the new government. Thus three Eurobonds worth 630 million dollars which had become due for payment have been exchanged by the Musharraf government with new Eurobonds at a higher interest rate of ten per cent with six years' maturity.

The rescheduling arrangements are due to expire on 31 December 2000 and debt servicing in the fiscal year 2001 is projected at five billion dollars. However, Musharraf and Finance Minister Shaukat Aziz have signalled that Pakistan would like to negotiate another rescheduling beyond December 2000.

In the last fifty-two years, Pakistan has sown seeds of discontent, social and regional inequities and institutionalised the rule of a civil and military bureaucracy sharing power off and on, with a handful of feudal lords and industrial barons. It has lived beyond its means for twenty-five years incurring foreign and national debt that equals its gross domestic product. Its corruption and dependence on foreign aid is legendary. Its economy is being sustained by debtors scared of the chaotic scenario that would engulf the region should Pakistan also go to the mat, like Iran did in 1979 and Afghanistan has recently.

The Musharraf government is currently faced with two options — move towards a civilian rule, as is being demanded by the Western countries, or launch a crackdown on the corrupt who abound among the interest groups controlling the present unequal system in Pakistan. An Islamabad-based magazine summed it up when it proclaimed on its cover a month after Musharraf's coup: 'The coup has arrived, the revolution is awaited.'

# Will Two and Two Equal Five?

## PAMELA CONSTABLE

The South Asia bureau chief of the *Washington Post* on what Musharraf can learn from foreign dictators — Chile's Pinochet and Turkey's Ataturk — and on whether he can succeed in his mission.

*Like Musharraf, Pinochet too came in promising to restore democracy but stayed on for seventeen years.*

This is not martial law, it is only another path towards democracy.

— *Gen. Pervez Musharraf*

The worst democracy is better than the best martial law.

— *Dawood Hassan*, Lahore shopkeeper

On 17 October 1999, when Gen. Pervez Musharraf appeared before the television cameras as Pakistan's self-appointed military chief executive, he exuded a sense of sombre, patriotic determination to save his country from civilian-led chaos and corruption.

Dressed in crisp khakis and seated beneath a portrait of Pakistan's revered civilian founder, Mohammed Ali Jinnah, the fifty-three-year-old Musharraf spoke of a nation whose irresponsible elected leaders had betrayed Jinnah's vision, leaving Pakistan's public institutions in disrepute and offering its citizens only a 'sham' democracy. Now, he said, the army had no choice but to step in and thoroughly cleanse the system. 'This is not martial law, only another path towards democracy,' he declared.

As I watched Musharraf, I was impressed by both his message and manner. As a newcomer to South and Central Asia, I knew little about Pakistan's past experience under military rule except what I had read in books and journals. But there was something unsettlingly familiar about the general's performance, something that instantly took me back to an earlier era in a distant part of the globe. I suddenly realised that like many people in Pakistan, I, too, had heard it all before.

On 11 September 1973, in Santiago, Chile, another robust, greying army general seized power from a controversial elected government. He told the nation he had no choice but to step in and save his country from economic ruin, from squabbling politicians, from the folly of failed democratic rule. His name was Augusto Pinochet Ugarte.

Like Musharraf, Pinochet was the product of a proud and disciplined institution. He too, started out with a vision of cleansing and modernising society; of creating a democracy in which the public would directly participate without the tainted interference of self-serving politicians. And as in Pakistan, the army's seizure of power was welcomed with relief by a sizeable segment of the Chilean populace, which had become disillusioned with democratic rule but assumed the armed forces would remain in power only as long as it took to restore order and tranquillity.

'I don't want to appear to be an irreplaceable person. I have no aspiration but to serve my country,' declared Pinochet, soon after overthrowing socialist president Salvador Allende and unleashing a wave of repression against leftist party activists. 'Our duty is to give form to a new democracy,' he said, a strong and modern system that would protect citizens from demagoguery and violence. 'As soon as the country recuperates,' Pinochet vowed, the military would hand over the reins of government to 'whomever the people desire.'

Instead, Pinochet was to remain in power for seventeen years, and Chile, which had known nearly a century of stable democratic rule, was to undergo Draconian change. The coup, a product of mass ideological confrontation rather than a personal showdown between two men, was both vengeful and cruel. Determined to punish the left and 'extirpate' its influence from Chilean soil, Pinochet's regime banned all political activity and rounded up tens of thousands of socialist and communist activists. Many were gruesomely tortured by a newly-created secret police, and more than three thousand vanished in custody. To make matters worse, a former leftist Chilean diplomat was assassinated in Washington, D.C. by Pinochet's agents, turning the regime into an international pariah.

At the same time, the regime instituted a series of drastic economic reforms aimed at lowering inflation, shrinking the public sector and transforming an inefficient sheltered economy into a globally competitive one. As the bitter economic medicine began to work, hundreds of thousands of people lost their jobs and their dignity, while a new breed of ambitious, military-nurtured entrepreneurs replaced the modest, public-minded middle class that had always distinguished this small Andean republic.

After a full decade in power, Pinochet began to face mounting public pressure that gradually forced him to open up the political system. And as the economy began to respond to the severe prescriptions of his American-educated neoliberal economic team, the regime became increasingly identified with economic success rather than political repression. When he finally left office in 1991, having been narrowly defeated in a national plebiscite, Pinochet was convinced he would be remembered in history as a patriot who had saved his country from communist chaos and implanted a modern, global economy in its place.

Instead, the eighty-five-year-old retired general now faces a humiliating court battle in two continents. In an unprecedented legal move with potential implications for former dictators the world over, the Spanish courts have sued Pinochet on behalf of human rights victims from the 1970s. The case has kept the unrepentant and ailing general in British custody for many months, and he may now have to return to Chile and face trial there.

As Pinochet's legacy is examined with the dispassion of time, it seems glaringly mixed: a traditional economy was successfully transformed into a modern one, but at a cost of trampled human rights and needless humiliation. Under Pinochet, a nation's bitter divisions were frozen rather than healed by years of military control, and a proud professional army was perverted by a secretive, corrupting new role as domestic secret police.

During repeated stays in Chile as a journalist and research fellow in the 1980s, I studied every aspect of Pinochet's rule. I listened to his speeches and interviewed his aides. I met former political prisoners and ambitious businessmen and jobless public servants. I visited fishing villages and copper mines, flea markets and flashy boutiques and respectable parlours in Santiago, learning about the victims and beneficiaries of dictatorship.

I saw how a professional and disciplined military ruler, who weighed advice carefully and chose a firm path, could make necessary but drastic changes in the economy and government structure that a civilian politician would never have dared attempt. But I also saw how a single military ruler, with no checks or balances on his absolute power, could succumb to the temptations of messianism, needless cruelty and a dangerously misplaced conviction that he had become permanently indispensable.

Now, as the excesses of Pinochet's rule returned to haunt him a quarter-century later, a new military regime had been born in Pakistan. As I listened to Musharraf's first speech in Islamabad on 17 October, I felt that Pakistan was facing a similar crossroads in its history like Chile had in 1973. Musharraf was starting out with many of the same patriotic motives and political advantages as Pinochet — but I could not help but wonder if his hopeful experiment might one day meet a similar fate.

Pakistan in 1999 and Chile in 1973 could hardly have been more different: one was a 150-year-old Roman Catholic republic with a history of strong political parties and vigorous debate, the other a new Muslim nation with weak civilian institutions that had only recently emerged from dictatorship. The events that precipitated the coups were different too; Chilean democracy was bedevilled by the ideological excess of revolutionary politics, Pakistani democracy by the paranoia of autocratic leaders and the greed of a corrupt economic elite.

There were also important distinctions between the military establishments that seized command of Chile in 1973 and Pakistan in 1999. Chile's army was a professional, Prussian-modelled institution with a long history of deference to civilian supremacy; it was Spartan in its ethos and isolated from foreign adversaries by ocean and mountains. Pakistan's was a politicised military corps that had intervened repeatedly in civilian affairs since the country's founding in 1947; it was a powerful and privileged establishment tinged with religious fervour and crucial to a country surrounded by potential enemies.

Yet there were also important similarities in these two situations — in both cases, the new regimes enjoyed a surprising degree of international support: in Chile, the US had encouraged the coup and ignored military atrocities in the name of anti-communism; in Pakistan, Washington has publicly protested but privately accepted the new regime as the country's best chance for stability and reform.

Perhaps in both the abuses and achievements of Pinochet's seventeen-year-rule in Chile — as well as in the shorter-lived, closer-to-home examples of previous Pakistani dictators Gen. Ayub Khan, Gen. Zia ul-Haq and the Turkish military ruler Kemal Ataturk — there are some important lessons for Musharraf to emulate and avoid as he takes on his own daunting, self-appointed and almost contradictory task as a military saviour of democracy.

'I feel like this is my country's last chance.' Maleeha Lodhi, the elegant but tough-minded editor of the *News International* in Islamabad, was explaining to me why she decided to accept a position as Musharraf's ambassador to the US. 'My whole life I have opposed military rule,' said Lodhi, a leader of Pakistan's liberal intelligentsia whose last stint in Washington had been as ambassador for the left-leaning government of Prime Minister Benazir Bhutto in the early 1990s. Now, she declared, 'I have decided to put my career on the line, because I think the military are our last chance to reform or perish.'

Lodhi's reasoning was stark. A series of civilian governments, led by a 'narrow political elite,' had left many Pakistanis disgusted and disenchanted with democracy itself, she said. The country now faced a paradoxical choice between 'a liberal military government and an illiberal democracy.' For now, she said, 'reform and accountability must come first before we can have a playing field for democracy. I only hope that when it does come back, people won't use it again to loot and plunder the country.'

She was not alone in her assessment. In the weeks that followed Pakistan's military coup, most of the country's liberal opinion-makers fell into line — partly because they genuinely hoped Musharraf could bring about the desperately needed changes that successive civilian regimes had utterly failed to deliver; partly because they feared that the only remaining alternative to military tutelage was a fundamentalist Islamic revolution; and partly out of a pragmatic realisation that the army was back to stay for the time being, and it was better to be part of the winning team than a carping outsider.

The only point that kept sceptical Pakistanis from full-fledged endorsement of Musharraf was his refusal to announce any timetable for a return to democracy. Like Pinochet, who often invoked a mantra of '*metas, no plazos*' — Spanish for 'goals, not schedules' — Musharraf set no limit on how long Pakistan would remain under military control. That, he said, would depend on how long it took to thoroughly cleanse the system of corruption and create a 'truly representative' demo-cracy — presumably one in which the discredited reigning political elite had no part.

But rather than ringing alarm bells, many Pakistani experts found a variety of rationales for Musharraf's reluctance to commit himself to any deadline for military withdrawal. His-torical analysts suggested the general was wise to avoid the 'error' committed by General Zia in 1977, when he had pledged to hold elections in ninety days and then remained in power for eleven years (as if the 'error' had been the promise, not its betrayal). Constitutional lawyers rushed to point out that even if parliament and the constitution were suspended, at least they had not been dissolved, and that the press and courts were still being allowed to function.

'We should all be bothered about the lack of a timetable, but the public doesn't want one now, and they won't unless things start to go wrong,' said Najam Sethi, the editor of a leading weekly newspaper, *Friday Times*. Sethi too wished Musharraf well, saying, 'He must succeed, he must make tough decisions fast and resist the advice of the status-quo wallahs.' If Musharraf's reformist mission stumbles, Sethi warned, 'The propertied classes may revolt, the people may give up on modern secularism and turn towards Islam, and his own colleagues may decide to go further along the military route.'

The public, so far, has been relieved that there were no combat troops in the streets and no announcements of Draconian Islamic punishments, both of which accompanied the nation's last military takeover by General Zia in 1977. Moreover, Pakistanis were accustomed to seeing the army in power, and many harboured fond memories of military rule under General Ayub (1958-69) and General Zia (1977-88) as periods of economic growth and political tranquillity.

In contrast, during times when political democracy held sway in the capital and members of parliament debated policies and issues among themselves, the day-to-day experiences of ordinary Pakistanis had often been governed by the harsher realities of feudal or religious power. Most recently of all, the government of Nawaz Sharif had increasingly acquired the tenor of dictatorship, with virtually all institutional checks and balances, from courts to parliament, gradually emasculated as Sharif consolidated his grip on personal power.

For many Pakistanis, the struggle for economic survival, and the sense of being abandoned and manipulated by a corrupt political system, have become far more relevant issues than the preservation of a democratic system. Unlike India, where millions of poor people live in desperate conditions but feel they have at least some access to political or social represen-tation, large numbers of Pakistanis are alienated from demo-cratic politics and have come to view it, not without reason, as a process that involves and benefits only a small minority.

Pakistanis, wrote Indian columnist Kuldip Nayar shortly after the October coup, 'have a commitment of sorts to demo-cracy. But feudalism and fundamentalism have fashioned in Pakistan a culture which rationalises dictation and defends obedience. Over the years, they have stopped differentiating between what is right and what is wrong,' he wrote. 'High-handed and arbitrary actions have been carried out with impunity. The nation is in such a stupor that it has not realised the full implications of military rule.'

The public was also thrilled by Musharraf's high-profile crusade to crack down on fat-cat financial scofflaws, many of whom had been dining handsomely at the trough of a corrupt *rentier* state — while most Pakistanis could not afford to send their children to school. Soon after taking power, Musharraf announced that large-scale loan defaulters and tax evaders had one month to pay up or face arrest and prosecution. There was a small flurry of penitent calls to Pakistani bankers, but by the 16 November deadline, only a fraction of the money had been recovered. The next day, when army troops fanned through wealthy neighbourhoods in three major cities, arresting some of the country's most untouchable figures in politics and industry, the stunned nation practically wept in gratitude.

'I can scarcely believe it. The clouds have lifted and the sunny uplands beckon from afar,' gushed Ayaz Amir, a respected and usually sardonic columnist for *Dawn* newspaper. In just twenty-four hours, he wrote, the new government had dissipated years of cynicism and despair in a nation that had come to expect only hypocritical pieties and vindictively selective reforms from a kleptocratic ruling elite. 'To ears used to hearing weak porridge churned in the name of accountability, this is thundering music.... March on in this fashion, Great Chief, and troops of angels will speed you on your way.'

Pakistan's new military ruler seems well-prepared to take on a number of self-appointed and desperately needed missions, and he has named a number of largely well-respected experts and former officials to assist him. Like Pinochet, who wisely recognised his lack of expertise in a wide range of economic and social subjects, he seems both willing and eager to enlist the advice of seasoned and honest experts from various political backgrounds.

So far, moreover, Musharraf's pursuit of financial and institutional reform has been assiduously impartial: high-ranking debtors from all parties and power centres have been arrested, including former chief ministers, members of parliament and leading industrialists. In the new Cabinet and provincial administrations, officials have been appointed without regard to influence or political access. In the province of Balochistan, for example, one international development expert commented with surprised pleasure that after years of fending off aggressively corrupt local officials who tried to exact bribes and favours, he suddenly found himself dealing with a new crop of appointees who seemed scrupulously honest and public-minded.

But unlike Chile, which enjoyed a tradition of responsible bureaucracy that was largely free of corruption, Pakistan's

*Musharraf faces a paradox in every sector of public life.*

government institutions have a history of deeply entrenched corruption that all observers agree will be extremely difficult to root out. Virtually every transaction that passes through official hands, from installing a telephone to acquiring an export license, has long been obtainable only through bribes. The system itself is not geared to public service, but to personal gain, and people who actually pay their taxes or follow the web of government regulations are regarded as fools.

As he tackles such problems, Musharraf faces a paradox in every sector of public life. He wants to reform the government, but he must rely on the very bureaucracy that turned it into a machine for graft; he seeks to clean up a corrupt business climate, but doing so may alienate the industrial elite and its foreign partners; he hopes to create an effective and impartial political system, but its best and brightest members have given democracy a bad name. To truly prove he means business,

**139**

moreover, Musharraf will eventually have to gore the oxen of some influential and corrupt colonels and generals whose support he needs to maintain control of his own institution — a step some observers say he will be extremely reluctant to take.

If Musharraf is serious about making fundamental modernising reforms in Pakistan, he must also take on its feudal system. Unlike Chile, which had already undergone a sweeping land reform when Pinochet took power, Pakistan's economic resources and political power are still largely in the hands of a landed rural elite, which systematically prevents large segments of the population from acquiring education or political rights.

Even a liberal leader like Benazir Bhutto was a feudal who never touched the basic equation of rural power, while Nawaz Sharif, initially hailed as an industrialist who would break the feudal mould, instead embraced its leaders as political partners. Perhaps only a military man can challenge this formidable obstacle to change, but even Musharraf would face enormous pressure not to rock the feudal boat.

Finally, there is another element of Pakistani society, one whose power is rooted in emotional loyalty and spiritual inspiration, that the new military regime may be even less equipped to confront. In Chile, the major threat to mainstream democracy was the ideological fervour of Marxism. In Pakistan, it is the religious fervour of Islam. After fifty-two years as an Islamic state, Pakistan has still not found its identity or place in the spectrum of secular and religious values.

Dozens of Islamic organisations, some of them extremist and violent, operate in Pakistan today. Their electoral pull is weak, because their supporters tend to disdain democratic processes, but their mosque-based organisations are strong, their popular appeal is deep and their message is constantly reinforced by both government neglect at home and pan-Islamic fundamentalism in the region.

Children denied an education in Pakistan's abysmally under-funded public school system are welcomed in free Islamic academies (madrassas) in such cities as Peshawar and Karachi, where they memorise the Koran and are indoctrinated in the military tactics of jehad.

Sunni and Shia groups, vying for supremacy in the murky world of mosque politics, periodically unleash waves of horrifying sectarian violence. Islamic guerrilla groups such as Lashkar-e-Toeba, which recruit and train Pakistani youths to fight inside Indian-held Kashmir, keep the jehadist fervour burning and command widespread support for their crusade. Pakistan's madrassas were also the breeding ground for Islamic insurgents fighting against the Soviets in Afghanistan during the 1980s, and ties between Pakistani Muslims and the current Islamic regime in Kabul, the fundamentalist Taliban militia, remain strong. For some Pakistanis, Osama Bin Laden, the jehadist Saudi financier and alleged international terrorist being sheltered by the Taliban, is a hero.

From the outset, Musharraf has laid down markers in the looming battle for the soul of Pakistan state. In his 17 October speech, he called for the society to embrace a moderate version of Islam, warned that extremist violence in its name would not be tolerated, and said he hoped to see a 'truly representative government' in next-door Afghanistan, which is ruled by the radical Islamic, Pakistani-bred Taliban militia. But it will be very difficult for Musharraf to implement this vision in a society where radical Islam has already taken deep root, where his own military establishment is adamantly committed to the fight over Kashmir, and where his regime lacks the public and secular legitimacy of an electoral mandate.

Already the extremist groups are flexing their muscles: six rockets were fired at the American embassy and other international buildings in Islamabad after United Nations' sanctions were imposed against Afghanistan in November. Some radical Muslim leaders strongly denounced Musharraf after he praised Kemal Ataturk, the visionary Turkish military ruler of the 1920s who used his power to break various cultural and religious strangleholds on Turkey's progress, warning of dire consequences should he attempt the same kind of religious purge.

Moreover, there are many active and retired officers in the Pakistani military who sympathise with radical Islam and dream of a Shariat revolution — the transformation of society into a religious state ruled exclusively by Islamic Sharia law. Pakistan's military intelligence apparatus, a key player in military politics and an important source of institutional backing for any army chief, has a long and close relationship with Islamic insurgent groups operating both in Afghanistan and Indian Kashmir.

Musharraf himself was the senior officer in charge of Pakistan's military incursion into the Kargil mountains of Kashmir last summer. The surprise infiltration by Pakistan-backed insurgents led to a ten-week border war with India and helped precipitate the fatal showdown between Musharraf and Sharif after the prime minister ordered the fighters to withdraw. While calling for a negotiated solution to the Kashmir conflict, Musharraf has hastened to make it clear he is committed to the

Kashmiri cause, a sine qua non of Pakistan's army for half a century.

While there is no immediate threat to Pakistan's government from radical Islamic forces, their undeniable appeal to various segments of society places certain limits on what even a military ruler can do. Were Musharraf to show any signs of weakness on Kashmir, or make any questionable concessions to India in the search for statesmanlike stature, his days as the top commander in a military regime might be immediately numbered. Moreover, if he were forced to crack down on an outbreak of sectarian violence or terrorism, incurring the wrath of a powerful and radical clergy, Musharraf's bloodless coup could well be eclipsed by a bloody holocaust.

There are encouraging signs that this time will be different, that this dictator will not succumb to the temptations of vendetta or excess, and that Pakistan's army has become too worldly — and too aware of the country's desperate need for Western financial support — to resort to the thuggery and theft that would bring down the kind of international opprobrium Musharraf's bloodless, popular coup has initially escaped.

Musharraf, from all descriptions, is both serious in purpose and moderate in character. He is a career artillery officer and former commando squad leader, but he also enjoys Western music, speaks several foreign languages (his late father was a career diplomat who served in numerous posts abroad, including Turkey), and has a personal abhorrence to Islamic fundamentalism. He is also a 'Mohajir' — an immigrant whose family came from India after the turbulent 1947 partition of the two countries — in an army dominated by Punjabis, which makes him less beholden to the traditional (and partly corrupt) military elite.

Musharraf has said repeatedly that his personal role model is the Turkish leader Ataturk. Within less than five years, Ataturk forcibly freed his country from the tradition-bound Ottoman Empire rule of sultans, caliphs and mullahs, and transformed it into a modern constitutional state. With successive strokes of his pen, Ataturk abolished the sultanate, declared Turkey a secular republic, separated church and state, ordered the complete emancipation of women, and changed the national written language from Arabic to Latin script.

Although his motives remained patriotic and progressive, and his legacy is undisputed as the visionary founder of a modern state, Ataturk's methods were dictatorial and occasionally cruel. Musharraf's endorsement of such a leader has aroused furious criticism by some Islamic leaders, forcing him to beat a somewhat hasty tactical retreat. 'Yes, I admire him. Now everyone thinks I am going to follow everything that he did. Obviously not,' the general told *Newsline* magazine in November. 'He did something in Turkey in a different environment. My role model is really the Quaid-e-Azam (Jinnah).'

Although Musharraf faces no immediate political enemy, he may well be tempted to use repression if his initial honeymoon sours and his regime begins to incur public criticism and protest. For now, the notion of wiping out partisan politics has great appeal in Pakistan, and Musharraf's stated desire to create a new, improved political system has been widely welcomed. But is it possible — or truly desirable? Pakistan has been failed by its top elected leaders, and it has not nurtured a younger generation of activists to replace them. Its parties are young, weak, and personalised, and they need to be developed into functioning institutions that do not depend on a single powerful leader. But to take root, this desperately needed reform must come from within, not from above.

If Musharraf wants to create a 'truly representative' democracy, he must find a way to strengthen, not weaken, the existing political system. The political gene pool must be broadened to include Pakistanis from all walks of life, not just the incestuous moneyed elite that has controlled it until now. The press must be allowed to raise all public issues — as the new regime, to its credit, has permitted thus far. The Constitution should be redrawn to undo some of the undemocratic damage wrought by Sharif, and to re-introduce some basic institutional checks and balances. But can any military regime, even the best-intentioned, democratise a system by executive fiat? History, in fact, suggests that the effect of long-term military rule is usually the opposite.

'An army can exercise power, but it provides a poor substitute for governance,' Paula Newberg, a Washington-based expert on South Asia, wrote in November. Government by edict, 'enforced at the barrel of a gun, may provide order, but it evades the real meaning of law,' she wrote. While lauding Musharraf's call for accountability as 'commendable,' Newberg warned that accountability must not be simply a narrow 'regime of punishments' but a comprehensive system of public life. Otherwise, she suggested, such efforts inevitably become reduced to 'minor posturing' and 'weaken political society so thoroughly' that they 'virtually guarantee the failure of civilian governments that try to follow military rule.'

It is entirely understandable that few Pakistanis today are mourning the enforced eclipse of the country's two major political parties and their leaders. The decade-long, see-sawing power game between Nawaz Sharif and Benazir Bhutto is widely blamed for having discredited democracy itself. Yet no one seems in a hurry to locate or groom younger, untainted leaders who could begin refurbishing democracy's image now, be prepared to fight if military rule becomes overbearing, and be able to compete fairly for power when it ultimately ends. The longer this situation persists, the easier it could become for Pakistan's military rulers to justify an ever-lengthening postponement of the promised return to civilian rule.

Moreover, despite his repeated insistence that he seeks to improve and restore democracy as soon as possible, Musharraf has already assumed some instantly recognisable traits of a dictator. Like Pinochet, who was named after a Roman emperor and who often spoke of 'my borders' and 'my mission' to save Chile, Musharraf slides a bit too seamlessly into the first-person-singular when talking about his regime's plans and policies. In a typical interview with *Time* magazine in early December, he began virtually every answer with the pronoun 'I.' Would the Constitution be amended? 'I haven't decided as yet.' Would a public referendum be called? 'I am not considering a referendum at the moment.'

Even one of the most respected and eloquent unofficial ambassadors for Musharraf, former army chief and foreign minister Sahabzada Yaqub Ali Khan, has expressed serious personal doubts about the ability of any military regime to act as a successful midwife to democracy — especially one that faces such multiple and powerful obstacles to change as Pakistan does: an entrenched feudal elite, a corrupt bureaucracy, a radical Islamic clergy and a weak federation of state governments with little loyalty to the centre.

'I can't help posing the question: when you ask a military regime to give way to democracy, are you asking the impossible?' Khan wondered in a recent conversation with me. 'It has nothing to do with Musharraf,' or the character of any other military ruler, he suggested. 'What is the DNA of that child? What star is it born under? How can you expect a baby delivered of martial law to produce its opposite? Are we asking two and two to equal five?'

Technically, Musharraf's rule may not fall into the category of full martial law — as the general has pointed out repeatedly — but for all intents and purposes, there is no question that one man, and one man alone, is calling the shots in Pakistan. And unless that man proves to be exceptionally wise and independent — after a twenty-five-year rise through the ranks of an institution that rewarded blind obedience and loyalty to group tradition — Pervez Musharraf could well be another Augusto Pinochet in the making.

# Pity the Nation

## JASON BURKE

The former
South Asia
correspondent
of the *Observer*,
London on how
Pakistan needs
sympathy, and
why India
needs to find
the necessary
compassion
and generosity
to do that.

It is mid-afternoon on 28 May 1998. Mohammed Amin, a grey-bearded Baluchi shepherd, is sitting in the shade of a desiccated wild olive tree watching a herd of goats — only eighteen of them left now after that accident with Ghulam Nabi's jeep — forage among the dry rocks deep in the hills on Pakistan's Afghan border. Two of the goats are his, the rest belong to his neighbours. This week it is his turn to take them out onto the bleached, gravelly slopes which are the nearest thing to pasture in about a hundred square miles of his small village. It is very hot. Mohammed Amin feels drowsy and his mind starts to wander. Ghulam Nabi sold his sister to Nisar Hyder Khan, he remembers. She was a beautiful girl. And he smuggled that container load of air-conditioning units in over the border last year. That's how he must have got the money for the jeep.

At 3.22 p.m. plus the time it takes for a shockwave registering 4.9 on the Richter scale to travel thirty miles, Mohammed Amin wakes up to find the ground shaking around him. He grabs for his stick and his pattu (blanket) but when he tries to stand up he can't find his footing and pitches forward onto the stones. With his face to the hard soil he mutters a blessing: 'Allah... Bismillah....' The moisture of his lips picks up the dust. After a few seconds he hears the dull boom of a distant explosion.

In Quetta, the dusty desert city 150 miles away, the tremor is felt a little less and a little later. But it is felt. It is felt by the man from the BBC, by the city's 350,000 inhabitants, by the Western oil prospectors corralled in the five-star Serena hotel, by the Pakistani scientists staying in a neat, whitewashed building in the sprawling army cantonment and by the small group of highly trained men from British intelligence who, as soon as the news reached London that the Indians had set off five nuclear devices in the Rajasthani desert ten days earlier, were sent to set up a listening station as close to the Pakistani nuclear testing ground as they could get. And above it all, the American spy satellites which had been scanning southwest Pakistan metre by metre for days picked out a cloud of dust and confirmed to the Central Intelligence Agency (CIA) who confirmed to the National Security Council who confirmed to the US president what Mohammed Amin could have told him, a little less technically but a lot more cheaply. The earth was shaking. Pakistan had detonated a nuclear bomb.

Where I was, at a desk in an office in the capital city of Islamabad, we felt no shockwave — at least not physically. In fact, my overwhelming emotion was that of relief. About two hours earlier, I had spoken to a local journalist. In an excited rush of Urdu and English, he had told me that Pakistan had finally responded to the Indian tests with a successfully completed test of their own. At least that is what I thought he had said and so I rang my newspaper in London to give them what I thought was a world exclusive. Unfortunately my Urdu, after two months in the country and a BBC *Get By in Urdu* course, was not quite as good as I had hoped. As I soon discovered, the reporter had just been saying that the tests were imminent, not completed. There followed a more than slightly worrying time as I wondered quite how to extricate myself from the mess before the first edition went to press. Then Nawaz Sharif came to the rescue and all was right with the world, or my world anyway. For the first, and almost certainly the last time, I wanted to kiss his shiny, bald pate.

Over the next few months Pakistan, and neighbouring Afghanistan, were the centre of the world's attention. A series of big stories broke like waves across the region. Pakistan tested again, hundreds died in a ferocious artillery battle in Kashmir, an earthquake rocked northern Afghanistan leaving five thousand dead. In August the Americans, hoping to kill Osama Bin Laden, who they held responsible for the bombing of their embassies in Kenya and Tanzania, fired seventy-five cruise missiles into the eastern Afghan mountains killing mainly goats and Pakistani teenagers. The Taliban militia launched a frighteningly successful blitzkrieg offensive, massacred several thousand unarmed civilians and nearly went to war with Iran.

It was only in the autumn of 1999, when the excitement died down and the stories were harder to come by, that I started to peer beneath the surface of the country I had been covering for six months. I found many things, some good, some bad. But they all seemed to be summed up in a poem written by Kahlil Gibran, the Syro-Lebanese mystical poet and artist, who died in 1931. He did not have Pakistan in mind when he wrote these lines but somehow seems to have written an epitaph for a country he could never have known. It is worth quoting in full.

> *Pity the nation that is full of beliefs and empty of religion;*
> *Pity the nation that acclaims the bully as hero, And deems the glittering conqueror beautiful;*
> *Pity the nation that only raises its voice, When it walks in a funeral, And will rebel only when its neck is laid, Between the sword and the block;*
> *Pity the nation whose sages are dumb with years, And whose strong men are yet in the cradle;*

*Pity the nation divided into fragments, Each fragment deeming itself a nation.*

I have now spent close to two years working in South Asia and nearly another year in total as a mountaineer. Around a third of the time has been spent in India, the rest in Pakistan or Afghanistan and there was one wonderful month in Nepal. I have watched the violent nationalistic tub-thumping of the nuclear tests mellow into the wary entente of the Lahore bus trip before reappearing like an obstinate cancer during Kargil and its aftermath. The blame is on both sides of the border though few would admit it. India is, undoubtedly, the bigger, stronger, more cohesive, more developed state. If Pakistan has been sinking fast for decades then India has been rising slowly. Even if General Musharraf does manage to turn the ship of state around, he is piloting an ailing supertanker not a yacht. India has little reason to be afraid of Pakistan. In part, this essay is an appeal to India, and Indians, to show what has been called 'the compassion of the strong.' Maybe that can lead to what De Gaulle called 'the peace of the strong.' Maybe India, and Indians, can find the necessary generosity. Maybe they too can pity the nation.

Just behind the flat I lived in when I first came to Islamabad is a plot of land covered in mimosa trees, wild cannabis and scrubby, prickly bushes. It is a graveyard and though no one tends it or comes to grieve at the dozen or so mounds of earth which lie among the rubbish under the trees, no one builds on it either — though the potential for profitable development of such a prime piece of urban real estate is high. It has been there for hundreds of years. The most modern and secular of Pakistan's cities has grown up around it and surrounded it with vast white palaces built by the nouveau riche and broad tree-lined roads and embassies and big private schools. It sits sadly among it all like a still, small reminder of an ever-intrusive past.

To one side of the graveyard, at least in winter when the trees die back, you can see the house of Benazir Bhutto, the former prime minister. It has twelve-foot walls, rumoured to have been built in deliberate defiance of planning regulations. Benazir has several homes in Pakistan but is currently in self-imposed exile in London. In April 1999 she was convicted of benefiting from huge financial kickbacks on government contracts awarded during her most recent term in office.

On the other side of the graveyard is the North Korean embassy. The North Koreans have supplied Pakistan with much of the technology that allowed them to detonate their bomb. Watching the embassy, and Benazir's house, and my flat, were usually two rather ineffectual looking intelligence agents. I knew them quite well after a while. They smiled sheepishly when greeted, like a neighbour who knows that you know about his recent affair with his secretary.

Half a mile away is the local market. In a purpose-built concrete and glass complex kebab vendors shout for custom and mobile vegetable salesmen weave overloaded bicycles through milling crowds. All the men wear shalwar-kameez. There are very few women. In the central square policemen lean their AK47s against walls and drink tea with their shackled prisoners squatting beside them. The lawyers sit under awnings in their open air offices and dictate letters to clerks who tap at ancient typewriters with little piles of empty tea cups at their elbows.

Around them the buildings are rotting slowly. Their exposed iron rods are rusty and the bright, white sun picks out the streaks of mould and the dirt smeared along their greying walls. It is the same throughout Islamabad. The rigid modern edges of the city have been eroded by three decades of exposure to the swarming reality of Pakistan as if by a weak acid solution. Islamabad's confidently certain lines, planned by a Danish architect in the 1960s, have, like anything certain in this region, and in Pakistan in particular, been bent and warped and the boundaries, like all boundaries in this part of the world, have been blurred.

Pakistan is a nation without borders, a land without true frontiers. A map of Pakistan, if accurate culturally, ethnically and religiously, would resemble a smudged charcoal sketch — a heavy thumb having smeared its northern frontier into Central Asia and substituted two indeterminate greasy stains for the clean black lines that supposedly divide it from Iran and Afghanistan to the west and India to the east. It is a country on the margin between the Middle East and the South Asian subcontinent and is truly a part of neither. Pakistan is fifty-two years old but, like a difficult adolescent, is still searching for a role and an image. Like a hungover partygoer — an inappropriate if helpful analogy in this dry and joyless land — Pakistan is caught in the long moment before basic points of orientation swim into focus. Pakistan's 'night before the morning after' was the mayhem of partition from India. The harsh lines drawn around it by British administrators who, having finished their work scuttled off to their semis in Surrey, disguise a messy reality. Five decades ago the swift, sharply new lines on the map provided little help to a confused nation rubbing its eyes in astonishment at its own existence. They provide little help today.

Though the British were, until the very end, opposed to Partition, Pakistan is nonetheless a legacy of their empire. If the British had never thought of unifying the subcontinent the concept of a separate homeland for its Muslims would never have occurred to the country's founders. The idea was entirely alien to most of the people on the land they hoped to hive off. Pakistan — the name means 'land of the pure' — was the conception of a very small number of rich, Westernised men who were entirely unrepresentative of the people whose future they decided. It was an artificial creation for which there was little popular demand. Fifty years ago the idea lacked broad-based mass support and it still does. Ask a Pathan tribesman

*A Pathan tribesman is loyal first to his tribe, secondly to his religion and thirdly to Pakistan.*

'We're not sure who we are but we are definitely not India
and we are definitely Muslim, we think.'

in Hangu or Darra Adam Khel or Dir about his allegiances and he will tell you that he is loyal first to his tribe, secondly to his religion and thirdly to Pakistan.

With such a gaping ideological vacuum at its core it is obvious why Pakistan has been forced to constantly define and redefine itself against India and around Islam. Though the national motto is 'Faith, Unity, Discipline', perhaps a more accurate substitute would be, 'We're not sure who we are but we are definitely not India and we are definitely Muslim, we think.' (One of the interesting things about General Musharraf is that he provides a coherent vision of Pakistan — as a modern, progressive Islamic state on the lines of Egypt or Turkey — for the first time in decades.)

The indoctrination starts early. When I joined Benazir on a visit to a school in her constituency deep in the rural south of the country, the children put on a play for her about a handful of outnumbered Pakistani soldiers in the 1965 war killing swathes of Indian soldiers before finally being over-powered. By the final scene the school's stage was almost entirely hidden by mounds of dead eight-year-olds.

Yet, though so often gazing with fear and fascination at the huge country on their eastern frontier, Pakistan's culture and religion also draw it in the other direction — towards the Middle East and Central Asia. In many ways Pakistan should be considered the easternmost fringe of the Middle East, rather than the western border of South Asia — just drive down the Shar-e-Faisal from Karachi airport with the city spreading out on either side looking like a dirty Dubai.

So, of course, there is Islam. The depth to which religion

**159**

articulates the responses, values and behaviour of the nation —
both at a personal, grassroots level and at a national and a
geopolitical level — is difficult to overemphasise. In the course
of two years I have interviewed innumerable aspirant ghazis
(holy warriors). All of them, with their wispy immature beards
and soft hands, reveal the same deep motivations. Like all
teenagers they want self-esteem and a sense of identity. And
the choice for them is relatively clear. They can look to the
West and aspire to secular democracy and liberal society and
MTV and jeans et al and feel, inevitably, second best. Or they
can turn to militant Islam and feel strong and powerful and
superior. When I spoke to young Lashkar-e-Toeba activists in
Muzaffarabad or visited the dingy Harkat ul-Ansar offices in
a narrow back street in Lahore and listened once again to the
now hackneyed calls for jehad and 'the blood of the oppressors
and crusaders', etc., the attractions of such an ideology for a
young lower-middle class, semi-educated Pakistani man
became obvious. And the nation as a whole is pursuing a similar
quest: for identity, for a role, for a feeling of self-worth.

One of the reasons for the outpouring of jingoism after
Pakistan tested its nuclear devices — the sweets distributed at
mosques, the chanting crowds shouting Allah-ho-Akbar and
parading rocket-shaped papier-mâché models with 'Islamic
Bomb' on the side through the streets of Karachi — was the
feeling that the test was a demonstration of the country's key role
as a leading nation in the 'Ummah' or Islamic world. And it is
not necessarily nationalistic hubris. Pakistan is the world's
second largest Muslim state with at least 130 million inhabitants.
It is in a key strategic position on the cusp of the Middle East.
Its Islamic universities draw from the whole Muslim world.

But the emphasis on Islam does not necessarily lead to

*Muslims kill more fellow Muslims in Pakistan than have ever died in India at the hands of Hindus or Sikhs at any time in the last five decades, excluding in Kashmir.*

greater nationalist cohesion. Again there are difficulties, contradictions and inconsistencies. There is as much diversity in Islam as there is in any religion and the differences between the views of the Sufi mystic I interviewed in the deserts of rural Sindh and the Sunni mullah who looked after me in the northwestern town of Kohat are very great. Muslims kill more fellow Muslims in Pakistan than have ever died in India at the hands of Hindus or Sikhs at any time in the last five decades, excluding in Kashmir. Doctrinal differences may not be the sole cause of the carnage but they are certainly a facilitating factor.

And the stress on the 'Ummah' tends to encourage international pan-Islamic loyalties which actually diminish the status of the individual nation state. Islam is not big on nation states. It is not a religion of petty nationalism or confrontation. It is, or should be, greater than that.

There are other ties to the Middle East beyond religion. Commercially Pakistan looks west. Decades of hostility with India has reduced trade between the two countries to a bare minimum. For twenty years the biggest foreign exchange earner has been the remittances of Pakistani workers in the Gulf. Whole villages in the northwest of the country are kept alive by cash sent back by family members working as drivers or labourers for Arab oil princelings. Economically, loans from the Arab states as much as from the Western-dominated multi-lateral lending bodies have been crucial in keeping Pakistan afloat. And historically, the bulk of invaders and settlers in Pakistan -- the Arabs, the Ghauris, the Huns, the Mughals — have come from the west. Thus most modern-day Pakistanis can — and often do — trace their roots back into Persia, Mesopotamia, Muslim Central Asia or further afield. Many of the crafts of Pakistan — glazed tiles, for example — reveal links to the Middle East. So does the Arabic in the language. Pakistan's greatest architectural monuments owe their lineage to the Islamic arts of Arabia, the Ottomans, the Ummayads and the Timurids. And the food: kebabs and nan bread are served, in one form or another, from Kashgar to Kuwait, from Hyderabad to the Hellespont. Significantly, if you ask for tea east of the Indus you are likely to be served black tea with milk, as you would be in India, Sri Lanka and Nepal. To the west of the river the tea is green and milkless as it is all the way west to Morocco. Sir Olaf Caroe, one of the greatest anthropological authorities on the region, said that Central Asia starts at the Margalla Pass, twenty miles west of Islamabad. And that was before the split from India.

The faultlines fissure across the country like the crazy web of cracks I watched splitting the earth during the Afghan earthquake in the summer of 1998. There are a dozen languages, scores of sects beyond the major division into Sunni and Shia, hundreds of tribes and subtribes, deep regional enmities, massive social divisions between the old feudal and the new commercial classes, cultural splits and a hundred thousand other bifurcations, dichotomies, schizophrenias, dilemmas. To coin a nuclear simile, Pakistan sometimes resembles a jumble of exploding neutrons held together in a cluster by only the weakest of ideological electrical forces.

One result of these centrifugal forces is that Pakistan is full of the sort of rhetoric one traditionally associates with slightly ludicrous South American dictatorships or Central African banana republics in the 1970s. Try a report of a clash on the Indian border, filed by the state-run news agency the Associated Press of Pakistan, for painfully overt jingoism. It doesn't matter when it was printed — I have read hundreds like it since I came to the country. They run in the papers almost every other day. It reads: 'Indian Attack Repulsed in Shyok Sector: The Pakistan army successfully repulsed an unprovoked attack on a forward post by Indian troops ... inflicting heavy casualties on the aggressor. The valiant Pakistani troops, displaying traditional courage and determination to defend every inch of the country's territory, thwarted the attack in which a large number of the (Indian) intruders were killed.'

India does, of course, oblige when an ogre is needed. During the Kargil crisis the Pakistani Army took me up the lovely Neelam valley. Among the fir trees beside bubbling mountain streams thousands of men, women and children were living in overcrowded tent villages. Though the sun was shining it was cold and ribbons of mountain fog blew across the valleys. They were spending the summer as refugees in the forests because their homes were being shelled by the Indians. We visited a hospital where three or four young boys lay strapped and trussed with tubes and bandages into military beds. The boys told us how Indian mortar shells had smashed into their playground killing their schoolmates. I don't think they were lying. Overhead the guns thudded dully. An hour later, machine-gun bullets from Indian positions on the other bank of the Neelam sprayed around our white, clearly civilian landcruiser and punctured the tyres of a clearly civilian, brightly painted truck ten metres away. Every wall in every village in the valley was shell scarred. Schools and hospitals lay destroyed. Whole settlements lay in ruins where the rubble was mixed with shards of ordnance. It seemed an insane way to fight a war — or win a propaganda battle for that matter. It still surprises me that India, usually so subtle, could so willingly supply ideal material — blown up babies, machine-gunned buses — for self-serving politicians and extremists to whip up hatred.

And with such appalling ignorance about each other on both sides of the border it is not hard to get the mobs charged up. Covering the Lahore bus trip one could see that all the Indian reporters present were overjoyed to find that (a) Pakistanis didn't have horns or little Kalashnikovs growing out of their heads and (b) that everyone was getting on so well. It was as if they expected to be strung from the nearest lamppost with a 'Free Kashmir' placard around their necks. Perhaps only North and South Koreans share so much and know as little about each other as contemporary Indians and Pakistanis.

I sat with a group of Pakistani junior army officers in a bunker a kilometre or so from the frontline during the last days of the Kargil conflict. Above us Indian shells rumbled through the air like distant trains and thumped heavily into the rocky hillside. In the bunker — the luxury dug-out that stood in as a makeshift mess and control room during heavy bombardments — we watched Zee TV and the South Asian edition of MTV. An officer who had recently come down from Siachen and still bore the tan and the scars turned to me and asked: 'What are Indians like?' To which the only honest answer was, 'Just like you.' Except they don't shout Allah-ho-Akbar when they fire their howitzers.

The bombastic rhetoric, the — to a European ear anyway — ridiculous patriotic songs, the gargantuan military parades and the models of the Ghauri missile or the Chagai hills that now litter Pakistan's urban landscape serve a purpose, however. The bottom line is that Pakistan needs something more than the hatred of India, Islam and the PIA (Pakistan International Airlines) to hold it together.

I'll bore you with a few statistics. Indians and Pakistanis take as much pleasure in reading statistics about each other as small boys proverbially do in comparing the size of their genitalia. Here goes anyway: around seventy per cent of the country's 130 million people can't read or write, nearly half of all families live in a single room, more than half have no sanitation or no clean water or neither. Violent crime — often sectarian — is endemic. The country has more than twenty billion pounds in public debt alone. One per cent of the population holds seventy per cent of the wealth. There are an estimated three million heroin addicts. The nation's population will double within twenty-five years.

And it is only when you drive through a hundred or so miles of Punjab countryside and see village after village — many without a single properly constructed building other than their mosque — that you start to realise the vast scale of the poverty and its appalling anonymity. Nothing new for an Indian, I am sure, but for me it only began to sink in when, after investigating a particularly nasty murder in one Punjabi village — the result of religious prejudice and poverty and seething village politics — I flew low over the region on the way back to Lahore and saw the grid of irrigation channels and the innumerable, regular clusters of houses scattered across the fields. Many of the villages or 'chaks' don't even have names. They are still known by the numerical designations given them by the British. So the dateline on my murder story was the rather bizarre looking 'Chak 100P'.

The poverty manifests itself in different ways. When last spring an oil tanker overturned trying to avoid a bullock cart on a main road near the central Punjabi city of Jhang, hundreds of villagers ran to it with buckets and bags to collect the spilling petrol. Inevitably, someone dropped a cigarette and the whole thing exploded in a fireball which killed fifty and injured a hundred more. Again no different from India, I suppose.

Even the violence here is infinitely diverse. There is the spectacular: the innumerable shoot-outs between warring political groups in the streets of Karachi, the 'encounters' between police and criminals which somehow always seem to end with a lot of corpses — suspiciously few of which are in uniform. There are the bomb blasts on trains (always blamed, possibly fairly, on the Indian secret service) and the grenades casually tossed by 'divinely inspired' teenagers into mosques crowded with those who happen to worship Allah in a slightly different way.

Then there is the boring, mundane violence that rarely makes the papers, much of it against women. Journalists and readers are so inured to it that when a teenage girl from the Pathan tribes of the North West Frontier is publicly executed for bringing shame on her family by being raped it merits a two-paragraph story on page twelve. For me the full page my newspaper gave to the story of one such girl, Lal Jamilla Mandokhel, was one of the most satisfying achievements of my time in the region so far.

Perhaps the most distressing part of the violence in Pakistan is that no one ever seems to be punished. The police

*The police in Pakistan do only four things well: corruptly make money, harass minorities, torture people and carry out extra-judicial murders.*

appear to be able to do only four things well: corruptly make money, harass ethnic and religious minorities, torture people and carry out extra judicial murders. Hundreds of people, no doubt many of them hardened criminals, have been shot dead by the police in rigged shoot-outs. Other crimes, however, are treated with slightly less severity, particularly if the criminal is rich or powerful and the victim isn't. Justice Abdul Majid Tiwana of the Lahore High Court said last year: 'Our judicial system has come to such a pass that none belonging to a privileged class can be asked by anyone in the country to account for his acts, however unlawful and reckless they may be ... This is because the system is meant to punish the less fortunate, the weaker and the helpless.'

So a man who pours acid into his wife's face because she wants to divorce him can bribe the police to arrest her relatives to stop them from filing a case against him. When a servant girl in one of the white mansions that pass for chic houses in Islamabad is raped by her employer, his son and four friends, the police are swiftly paid off and nothing happens. The girl is kicked out on to the street. Not so different from parts of northern India, in fact. In Chak 100P I found that when a member of parliament has the choice between backing an investigation into the fatal lynching of a defenceless old woman or protecting her killers he chooses the latter. The logic being that dead people don't vote.

In Africa you find the violence is brutal and chaotic. In Pakistan it is systematic and institutionalised. If you are poor or weak then there is no protection. If you have any element of strength you use it. In Pakistan the strong bully the weak and the weak bully the weaker. I had an insight into the mentality of Pakistan's rulers when, after publishing a detailed story in the *Observer* revealing that Nawaz Sharif owned four Park Lane apartments and had sent millions of dollars overseas, the prime minister's brother sent a car full of heavies to my flat.

I met an American-educated advertising executive on a plane to Karachi recently and asked him how he would sell his country to the rest of the world. He thought for a moment and then, absolutely deadpan, said his slogan would be, 'You Are Welcome To Pakistan.' He chuckled at his own joke for the rest of the flight.

Yet, as ever, the certainties shift and fade and rearrange themselves. In the scrubby, dusty, dirt poor hills of Dir, high up on the North West Frontier, I watched an opium farmer insist on slaughtering his few chickens so as to be able to properly feed the dozen soldiers and bureaucrats who had come to enforce a government directive and destroy his crop. They were there to force him and his ten children into poverty, yet he served them tea and biscuits himself. And even when I was arrested in Balochistan, trying to reach the Afghan border without a permit, the policemen who hauled me in insisted that I share their chapatis, kebabs and salad before interrogating me about my supposed activities as an American spy.

Throughout the country — although this doesn't seem to apply to bureaucrats or politicians — people want to help you out. They are willing to make massive enormous sacrifices to make your life easier, driving miles out of their way to take you to your destination, giving up days of their time to help you research a story that they will never see and couldn't even read if they did. And, with courtesy and consideration certainly very rare in the West and, I think, increasingly rare in India, they will

**169**

make even greater efforts to hide their sacrifice from you. And I have never, either in Pakistan or in Afghanistan, encountered any hostility as a Westerner. Throughout all the multitude of conversations about the role of the West whether with Marxist doctors in Karachi or with mullahs in Peshawar, impeccable courtesy was impeccably maintained.

In Afghanistan it borders on the ludicrous. While driving along the desert road from the southern Afghan city of Kandahar to Herat close to the Iranian border I was warned about bandits. After a brief discussion my driver decided we should stop — a hundred kilometres short of our destination — because it was getting dark. The problem was not my security, he said, but his own. The bandits would not harm me as I was a guest in their country. I did not believe him and kicked up a fuss before resigning myself to a chilly night wrapped in a single blanket on the terrace of a roadhouse tea stall or chaikhaana. Yet a week or so later I heard of a bus carrying two aidworkers which had been stopped by the bandits on the same stretch of road. They had robbed the locals of their worthless Afghanis and their cheap jewellery but hadn't touched the foreigners with their five hundred pound cameras and their wads of dollars. The same ethos governs the behaviour of the Pathans on the Pakistani side of the border.

Throughout Pakistan's short history others have been telling its people what they should do and be and think. As ever, as I have learned more about the country, I have realised how little I actually do know about its past, its future or what Pakistan is now. But I also came to realise that few Pakistanis had much of an idea either.

I arrived in Islamabad at the time of the great 'Urs' at Bari Imam. Bari Imam is a local saint and his shrine lies about a mile outside Islamabad near the large village of Nurpur Shahan. Every year there is a carnival — the 'Urs' — at the end of March to commemorate his death. I drove out to it on a hot spring evening in late March.

The road out from Islamabad winds through the diplomatic enclave — where the city's diplomats and immigration officials are corralled behind barbed wire and whitewashed walls — and then through wheat fields and scrub. The fields were very green in the evening light and the mud-walled houses of the village were pink and brown. Men and women were marching along the verges of the road in rough columns and the sun shone through the dust they raised and reflected off the drums and trumpets of the bands which led them. Each group carried huge flags in primary colours with tinsel wrapped round the staff. Many had walked for hundreds of miles. Some had bleeding feet which left spots of blood at each stride which dried quickly into iron coloured stains on the dusty tarmac.

I parked behind a checkpoint manned by a group of unusually cheerful blue-shirted Islamabad policemen and walked up the final five hundred metres to the shrine with the crowd. The pilgrims converged on the shrine like a football crowd, each group carrying a giant mock-up of either a ship or a mosque made out of multicoloured glass, innumerable pieces of mirrors and gaudy plastic. Down either side of the broad field leading into the village's main street stalls had been erected. The boys selling pappadums had stacked their eighteen-inch wide crumpled discs in piles a metre high. Other stalls offered smoking kebabs, garlands of deep pink flowers, shiny tinsel and foil hats. There were women hoping to henna hands, tables full of portraits of the dead saint himself — despite the Islamic injunction against human images —, huge piles of bangles glittering red and green and gold and neat stacks of halva puri. A strongman oiled his muscles while two assistants melo-dramatically manoeuvred his barbells into position in front of a crowd.

The shrine itself is a whitewashed mosque in a sunken courtyard with several large trees around it. It is set in a walled compound where hundreds of canopies and tents had been pitched by the pilgrims. There were cooking fires next to each tent around which groups of men squatted talking loudly in local dialects: Punjabi, Hindko, Pashto. A band played a thin reedy music. Goats were tethered to guy lines. Banners inscribed with religious slogans in Urdu were draped over the tents. And above it all the big, bright flags the pilgrims had carried from their home towns flapped in the evening breeze.

I wandered around very pleased with myself for finding so much 'genuine' South Asian colour. Then I clearly heard someone say, 'All right mate,' in a strong northern English accent. Grinning at me was a tall young Pakistani man in a dark shalwar kameez. He was a twenty-two-year-old taxi driver who now lived in Leeds and his name was Majid Khaliq. He was 'British born and bred,' he told me, too quickly. But he was also the son of Mohammed Khan who was the brother of Mohammed Nazir who was a farmer in the village of Handpur Kaloney, near Mirpur in 'Azaad' Kashmir and so was 'a Pakki too,' as he put it. And it was from Handpur Kaloney — well over a hundred miles away — that he had walked with fifty of his 'brothers' from the village a few days earlier.

When I asked him what a Leeds taxi driver was doing at the Bari Imam 'Urs', he laughed. 'I just love it here,' he said. 'It's just fookin' magic. It's like right good innit, eh? I walk round and I'm like proud and like it's just mental. Everywhere you look there's something mad going on. It's like I'm proud of everything here like because its not the West and it makes me feel proud like. It makes me feel different.'

A group of pilgrims invited us to sit with them. All the pilgrims kept to their own areas. It was only because he was with me, Majid said, that the men from Peshawar would allow him, a Punjabi, onto their patch. We wandered off around the compound past whirling dancers, a large crowd of women brawling to get their hands on free rice, a number of preachers and a man with an enormous quantity of iron chains draped around his neck. He was walking steadily around a fire with very wide eyes. We walked up the low hill behind the campsite. Two young Pakistani men, in smart white kurtas, approached us and spoke only to me in poor English. They were university students, they said. They did not glance at Majid, let alone talk to him.

From the hill we could see the seething encampment beneath us and behind it the hills darkening as the sun went down. To the east a few fireworks popped and crackled above the smoking bonfires around the campsite. Drums pattered out a thudding rhythm. Looking west Islamabad's straight lines were picked out by the streetlights flicking on, sector by sector and the white neo-Palladian colonnades of the prime minister's residence could be just picked out in the gloom. Big cars were streaming through the city's broad avenues and neon winked out at us.

If France has 'Marie-Ann' as a symbol and America Uncle Sam then Majid, sitting there gazing one way at the brave new world of Islamabad and then in the other at the tumult of Bari Imam's 'Urs', might serve as similar icon for Pakistan. He would be an unlikely, unpopular but appropriate choice. Like Majid, Pakistan doesn't really know what it wants or which way to look for inspiration. Does it want a future as a secular liberal democracy like India or the West? Or as some kind of a moderate Islamic fudge like Turkey, as no doubt General Musharraf would like? Or as a hardline theocratic state like Iran under Khomeini with all the violence and repression that would involve? Does it want rapprochement with its neighbours — and for that matter with the world community — or confrontation? Does it want to be more Westernised or would it prefer to retreat into Taliban-style reaction? In ways that no one in Pakistan would care to admit, India has a key role, perhaps the key role, in determining its future development.

When we went back to camp Majid and I watched the pilgrims dance around their model ships and temples to bless them with songs before lighting them up with candles and parading them through the compound. Then Majid asked, rather abruptly, if I wanted to leave. I sensed he didn't want me to see something. So I said I'd better get going and he seemed relieved. Intrigued as to what sort of bizarre ritual Majid was unhappy with me seeing I walked a little way back up the hill and scanned the compound for him. I spotted him with difficulty. All the men in the encampment had formed lines. Majid was kneeling in the first rank facing the setting sun, his palms turned towards his chest in the first motions of prayer.

# Military Medium

### SANKARSHAN THAKUR

During his three trips to Pakistan, the associate editor of the *Telegraph* saw Peshawar taken over by Afghans, Hayatabad taken over by guns and ganja and Benazir Bhutto and Nawaz Sharif taken over by the army.

Chacha said he was like a father to me. He would not let me go. 'In any case, I don't think the flight will leave, it never does at times like these,' he announced. 'I'll wait for you outside, you'll come back.' An ashen, monster of a storm was flaring above Peshawar. Rain and wind were about to stir a reckless cocktail of the elements. 'The plane won't go, you'll come back,' Chacha repeated as I bid goodbye, adamant I had to leave. Chacha's prophecy of my return would come true, but not that day. I had appointments to keep in Islamabad. Besides, the telex lines from Peshawar had proved as unreliable as promises that one of the mujahideen groups would smuggle me across into 'liberated' Afghanistan via Khyber Pass. I had a pile of rotting stories to file. I had to leave.

There was no one at the Pakistan International Airlines (PIA) counter, not even passengers. I enquired at the duty office and they said they had not called the flight yet. But they hadn't cancelled it either. 'There is low pressure turbulence in the area, the flight has come but it may not leave.' I could see Chacha beyond the glass panes, waiting. It annoyed me to see him there, as if his presence was holding up the flight.

Then, all of a sudden, there was a burst of commotion in the terminal. Two young soldiers entered carrying briefcases and behind them strode in a senior Pakistani Army officer, a brigadier. He walked straight to the PIA counter and asked about the flight's status. The PIA staff probably told him the same thing they told me but then I saw the brigadier shaking his head and asking to speak to someone higher-up. A phone was hurriedly brought to him and he made a short call. 'I have to go, I have to be in Islamabad this evening,' I heard him tell someone. His tone was flat and declarative. 'The flight has to leave, we can beat the storm.' He put the phone down, instructed the PIA personnel to ready the flight and left for a far corner of the terminal asking his two subordinates to check him in.

Five minutes later, the PIA Dornier was airborne with the brigadier, his soldiers, two old Pathans carrying sackloads of fabric, and me. No cabin crew — the space is too cramped and the flight too short. We flew an opaque sky, tempting the eye of the storm racing close behind us. Pilots in a Dornier aren't partitioned off from the passenger area so we could hear the nervous exchanges on the radio between the cockpit and the control tower as the tiny sixteen-seater got thwacked about in air. The Pathans had their rosaries out, I dug nails into the lifeline on my palm, the brigadier sat expressionless through the turbulence, leaving his men no option but to do likewise. We landed in Islamabad slashing flying time by ten minutes. There was a strong tailwind pushing the Dornier but I suspect the pilot too had exerted the throttle to stay adrift of the storm.

Hail came sweeping over Islamabad airport moments after we got into the terminal. I met the pilot in the lounge and he said we had run barely two minutes ahead of the low pressure core. 'I had refused to fly in such conditions but the brigadier was inisistent. There were no military planes available, he had me overruled. He had some important meeting that could not wait, something about the Afghan crisis.'

This was late April 1992. The Watan Party government of Dr Najibullah had just been ousted in Afghanistan; Kabul had at last fallen to the mujahideen. But the celebrations had been short-lived. Along with victory was born its terrible twin: a wild war of succession. Rival Afghan militias were lunging for power, playing *buzhkhashi* (a medieval Afghan game in which horse riders fight one another over the carcass of a sheep) over Kabul.

Gulbuddin Hekmatyar, Islamabad's pet Pushtoon, had burst the bottle and was pounding the Afghan capital from the south, irate that he hadn't been handed absolute power — he had only been given the prime ministership. Sigbatullah Mojaddedi and Burhanuddin Rabbani of the Afghan National Liberation Front would rotate the provisional presidency according to the Pakistan-brokered, UN-blessed peace formula.

The 'liberation' of Kabul was to have been a medallion on Prime Minister Nawaz Sharif's bosom but it was suddenly stained by fratricidal bloodletting between the rival warlords, Hekmatyar the most ambitious and ruthless of them. His blistering revolt against the peace settlement had poached egg on Sharif's face. International pressure for peace was mounting but the horse Pakistan had backed all the while had run amok. The brigadier had been sent to Peshawar with a message to the Hekmatyar camp. He was in a desperate hurry to relay the response to his bosses; he could brook no delays.

On the long drive into Islamabad from the airport, I wondered whether an Indian Army general would have been able to commandeer a commercial flight without making noise or news. I also wondered whether the army would have been such a key player in what was essentially a political and diplomatic affair. It was dark and thundery and wet and the traffic stood blocked on the approach to Islamabad, shivering on the rain-slicked road. The generals were on their way to meet the prime minister.

What would happen to Nawaz Sharif over Kargil in the summer of 1999 was happening to him over Kabul in the summer of 1992. He had lost hold over events. He was going about pretending to be grandmaster of the Afghan chessboard when he actually had his hands tied behind his back. When he travelled to Kabul to sign the accord that installed the muja-hideen, his minders accompanied him: army chief Gen. Asif Nawaz Janjua and the ISI boss Lt. Gen. Javed Nasir, both eager to embarrass their prime minister and underline their own ascendancy. Prodded by international pressure, Nawaz Sharif had come round to that view and persuaded the pro-Hekmatyar Pakistani Army and ISI to agree to the deal. On paper, Janjua and Nasir agreed to let the Mojaddedi-Rabbani combine assume reins but on the chessboard, they arranged a siege by Hekmatyar's forces. Nawaz Sharif was a pawn faking prowess. He said one thing, the army and the ISI did another.

Nawaz Sharif sent foreign minister Siddiq Kanju to nego-tiate a deal with Hekmatyar but the army and the ISI flagrantly sabotaged talks, feeding Hekmatyar's ambitions and arsenal. Nawaz Sharif promised Benon Sevan, the UN negotiator on Afghanistan, that Hekmatyar's guns would be silenced and, sure enough, Hekmatyar launched the bitterest rocket attacks on Kabul from his bases on the southern peripheries of the Afghan capital the following morning. I remember Benon Sevan returning from a meeting with Nawaz Sharif one afternoon, puce with anger. 'We do not know what to make of the Pakistani prime minister,' one of his staff told me. 'We suspect the prime minister does not know what his government is doing, or, if he does, he is helpless. He is not in control, we don't know who is.'

One afternoon in Peshawar, crossing into the gun-ridden Hekmatyar-held quarter of town, I had asked Chacha that question: Who's in control? I was only half expecting an answer but Chacha had it ready.

*'Peshawar is not run by Pathans, it is run by Afghans because they have the big guns.'*

'Nobody,' he said, 'and everybody. This is a tribal country, might is right. You have the gun, you have the men, you rule, you control. At the moment, we are being run by Afghans.' He pointed to the gunmen on the rooftops of buildings and in the bazaars. 'Look everywhere, Peshawar is not run by Pathans, it is run by Afghans because they have the big guns. The only other people with the big guns are the army and they are with these Afghans.'

Chacha looked upon the entire Peshawar operation — the raising of Afghan militias in preparation for an assault on Kabul — with a mixture of dread and disdain. He was an old world creature, schooled in the values of Khan Abdul Ghaffar Khan, Peshawar's disowned deity. He never spouted platitudes on

Ghaffar Khan or Gandhi or non-violence but he was suspicious of the politics of guns. 'We Pathans love our guns,' he used to say, 'look where they've got us.'

I had met him quite accidentally in a barber shop in the back alleys of Peshawar while trying to lose my tail. I had grown one immediately upon landing there and after four days in town, still hadn't managed to shake it off. The tail must have been at the airport to receive me but a young colonel I met on the flight from Islamabad had offered me a lift to the hotel. He had lost me even before he could find me. So he came to the hotel late that first night, knocked on my door, saw me, mumbled something apologetically about mistaken identities and slunk off. He was probably wanting to put a face on the name he had been assigned to watch. The next morning, he was in the hotel lounge, pretending to read a newspaper.

Somewhere between the lounge and the porch, he appointed himself my unwanted attaché. After that he went wherever I went, on his red Honda motorbike. It must have been a dull and tiresome job lumbering behind a journalist whose most clandestine activity in Peshawar was leaping down narrow lanes to give the bladder a break.

The barber's, I thought, would be a good place to snip him off. I went in for a haircut. He parked his Honda and walked in too, taking a vacant place in the waiting lounge and promptly burying himself in a magazine. 'Want a haircut?' the barber asked him, his scissors chip-chipping on my nape. 'No,' he replied bluntly, 'just came in to read the magazines.' The barber flicked his brow and went about his business as if nothing was odd about this. Pakistanis are perhaps used to visitors who don't explain themselves.

The man who was about to become Chacha was getting his

moustache trimmed in the next swivel, a Clarke Gable cut running close and thin over his upper lip. Apparently amused, he turned to me and asked, 'India se? (from India?)'

We got talking. Chacha was a retired engineer, his sons were in the carpet business and prospering. His daughters were both married abroad. His wife… 'Well, she cooks and knits and I like calling myself a gentleman of leisure.' He was seventy-five but trim and ramrod straight. The next morning, he came to my hotel in his elegant Peugeot. He insisted on driving me around. 'That is all I do in any case,' he said, 'Indians rarely come to these parts now.'

You found news wherever you went in Peshawar. The town was teeming with Afghan militiamen waiting their turn to join the raids on Kabul. They roved the bazaars; they lolled about in the chai-shops, Kalashnikovs slung on their chairs like satchels; they jammed the exchange counters of Yaadgaar Chowk, buying and selling Afghanis, arguably the most volatile currency on earth in addition to being the most worthless. It was traded by the sackful.

At four every afternoon, we would head past the cantonment to the Hezb-i-Islami's headquarters for Hekmatyar's daily press conference. It was a dreary settlement populated by armed men and squat mud mosques. Hekmatyar would speak to us on a tenuous one-way radio line from an unstated location close to Kabul; it was less a press conference, more his message to the world. He would daily condemn the mujahideen council that had taken over and swear to dislodge it in the name of the Almighty. Daily he would claim new victories, also in the name of the Almighty. He was fighting and he would win, with or without help from Pakistan. The day Sharif signed the accord in Kabul, Hekmatyar sounded livid; he called Sharif a traitor to the Afghan cause and flayed the Pakistani government to shreds. The audience — militiamen and local youngsters gathered on the terrace where the radio receiver was installed —clapped everytime Hekmatyar challenged Islamabad's authority and made dire threats. Kalashnikovs were brandished and the terrace trembled with bellicose cries of 'Allah-ho-Akbar.' Peshawar did not seem like a place in Pakistan, it was an anarchic tribal outpost. Nobody was in control.

Though he was always a shadow, the man on the Honda never bothered us. One morning, coming out of the hotel, I was tempted to invite him for breakfast; god knows at what hour he had arrived to wait for me to emerge. But Chacha dissuaded me. 'It would embarrass and compromise him, it may cost the poor man his job.'

I complained mildly about being followed so doggedly to an official in Islamabad who was friendly and gutsy enough to call an Indian home for dinner. 'Oh, I know you have been followed here too,' he said. 'Reciprocal measures. You do it to our people, we do it to you.' But senior journalists in Islamabad told me they do it as much to their own. 'We call them farishtas (angels),' one of them said, 'they are ever-present and you never know who has assigned them. Often it is not the government. Often it is the ISI or the army acting on their own. They even keep tabs on prime ministers and presidents.' But in a society where suspicion and mistrust are equally distributed, Indians are a little more equal.

My journalist friend suggested that Chacha too was a monitor attached to me. But Chacha never did anything that hurt me, then or later. The closest he came was wishing my flight didn't take off in that storm. Pakistan is a small pond, things ripple back and forth quickly. If Chacha had been reporting on me and our conversations in his Peugeot, I would perhaps not have been granted permission for subsequent visits.

My first crossing to Pakistan — to what was then only a semi-romantic idea forged by exaggerated doses of myth and censored history — was prompted by the death of dictatorship and the birth of democracy. Gen. Zia ul-Haq had been killed in an air crash and Benazir Bhutto had made a triumphant entry riding the near-holy ghost of her father. The Bhutto legend had burgeoned, fed by Zia's repression. Next to US green cards, Zulfiqar and Benazir were the biggest Pakistani craze in 1988. The evil that Bhutto did had been interred with his bones, the good lived after him. 'Jeeway Bhutto, Jaavey Zia' was the slogan Pakistan was pirouetting on, freed suddenly from the yoke of military dictatorship. The mood was like Rajiv Gandhi's sweeping victory in December 1984: euphoric and expectant. But in many ways it wasn't like Rajiv Gandhi's election at all. Rajiv was elected to power and he assumed prime ministership. In Benazir's case, it wasn't as simple. She too had been voted to power but she had to wait to be handed power. With the Mohajir Qaumi Mahaz (MQM), she had won 107 seats in what was then a 207-member National Assembly. But her majority was no guarantee to power. The Establishment, which in Pakistan has always meant not party-political authority but the army and its allies (the intelligence setup, the Jamaat-e-Islami, big businesses that profit from military dictatorships), took its time giving her the nod.

Ghulam Ishaq Khan, then president of Pakistan, was a creature of the Zia regime. He was reclusive and taciturn and

*President Ghulam Ishaq Khan (centre) was as suspicious of Benazir as she was of him. The two are seen with Rajiv Gandhi during his visit to Pakistan in 1988.*

maintainted a sinister proximity to the generals and Islamic fundamentalist groups. He was suspicious of the Pakistan People's Party (PPP); they were Zulfi Bhutto's people, enemies licking old wounds, perhaps even seeking retribution. (Benazir herself remained suspicious of the president through her truncated tenure. S.K. Singh, then India's high commissioner in Islamabad, told me that when Rajiv Gandhi was in Islamabad for his celebrated summit with Benazir, the latter suggested they talk all 'important business' while taking walks on the lawns because there might be bugs in her office.) The Nawaz Sharif-led Islamic Jamhoori Ittehad (IJI) had managed only fifty-one seats but there was still speculation, realistic speculation, that the IJI might be handed power, or, at least, time to muster a majority through defections. It was a clean verdict; the pall of intrigue and conspiracy that hung over Pakistan seemed unnecessary. But it had been deliberately crafted. *The Pakistan Times*, a government-supported English daily, reported midway through the declaration of results that the 'IJI is leading with ninety-two seats, PPP trails with seventy.' When all the results were out, another government-subsidised daily, *Siyasi Log*, headlined its lead: 'Nawaz Sharif will be Prime Minister.' The story said the IJI had secured 'secret support' from the MQM and independents and was in a position to stake claim to power. Journalists in Islamabad and Lahore began to speculate whether the delay in appointing Benazir was actually meant to give time to Nawaz Sharif to cobble a majority.

Day after day, uncertainty mounted. It was almost as if Pakistan were two nations. The streets of Karachi and Lahore were in raptures over a new era, Islamabad was eerily sullen and suspenseful. In Lahore and Karachi they thought they had become masters of their destiny again but the real masters were still in Islamabad and still in control of the nation's destiny. They were yet to give their verdict on the verdict of the people. Anxiety swelled around Benazir Bhutto's Niazi House camp headquarters in Islamabad, day after day the suspense mounted. Benazir was impatient but nervous; the delay was rankling her but she did not want to displease the Establishment. She, herself, did not complain. Despite her victory in the elections, all Pakistan was aware it was still upto the shadowy forces of the Establishment to hand over power to Benazir.

She was forever accompanied by Gen. Tikka Khan, her father's defence minister. The 'Butcher of Balochistan' had turned democracy's archangel. He was shrivelled as an ageing bird and made laconic statements about the strange ways of army generals. Their only worth was their richness of irony. Gen. Tikka Khan was as clueless as the rest. Will Benazir get a call or won't she? There was no word from Aiwan-e-Sadr, the imposing Presidential Palace which sits overlooking Islamabad, hawk-like.

During the days of uncertainty, I went to Lahore to see Mazhar Ali Khan, one of Pakistan's most respected intellectuals and editor of the leftwing weekly, *Viewpoint*. He was despondent despite the return of democracy. 'Nobody can be quite sure what will happen in Pakistan,' he said. 'Democracy for us is like a leaf in a storm.' Mazhar Ali Khan had suffered personally during the long years of military dictatorship. For years he hadn't met his son, Tariq Ali, who was in exile in England; he had been harassed for his liberal, anti-Islamist beliefs; *Viewpoint* itself had hiccupped through troubled times. 'It is good that democracy is getting another chance but when that will suddenly change nobody knows. Elected prime ministers can take office but they can also be bundled out.'

Benazir was eventually named prime minister. Democracy had returned to Pakistan after too long. The world was watching though what really mattered was that the US, which subsidised Pakistan hugely, was watching. It was too soon to subvert democracy. But the Establishment extracted a price anyhow. Benazir had to surrender the key foreign affairs portfolio to an outsider — Sahebzada Yakub Khan, foreign minister in Ghulam Ishaq Khan's Cabinet, continued to sit in Benazir's Cabinet and run Pakistan's external affairs.

And despite her accession to power, all Pakistan knew she could be thrown out any moment, which she was in less than two years. The Eighth Amendment, which empowered Pakistani presidents to cast an elected government in the dustbin, or worse places, was still part of the Constitution. Not that the Establishment necessarily needed the Eighth Amendment when it made a grab for power. Nawaz Sharif scrapped the amendment after securing a two-thirds mandate in 1997— a victory fashioned by Asif Ali Zardari who lubricated Benazir Bhutto's fall with oily scams whose stains have spread as far as Sussex — but it still did not help. The Establishment ejected him, Eighth Amendment or no.

A few days after Benazir Bhutto was installed prime minister, I went to Rawalpindi to meet Aijazul Haq, son of the late Pakistani dictator. He still occupied Army House, from where Gen. Pervez Musharraf now rules. Power had trundled a little down the road to Government House where Benazir Bhutto sat dismantling Zia's portraits but Aijazul spoke the language of a man just beginning to plot his part. 'We'll be back,' was the first thing he told me, throwing a crisp towel round his neck, 'we as in I and my father's vision. He was what Pakistan needs, a man who speaks with the authority of the Almighty and has the guts to implement it.'

We were in the outhouse of the sprawling colonial era bungalow. Aijazul had just finished his daily tenure on the squash courts; the outhouse was his changing room. He was built slighter than his father but he had hints of the same hooded eyes and he had begun to groom his father's trademark handlebar moustache. He was shy neither of what his father did nor of his own ambitions. 'There are people who respected my father and what he did,' he told me, 'they want a mantle bearer of General Zia's legacy and I am here.'

He could perhaps read the expression on my face as he said this; perhaps by some insight he divined I was mentally dismissing his statements like the fantasies of a semi-important fool even as I took notes. It was tough to take him seriously at that time. Zia was a reviled man in the Pakistan of 1988. He had been buried unmourned, Zulfi Bhutto had been resurrected.

Aijazul nodded to himself and wagged his forefinger at me and said, 'You are Indian so you will have problems understanding the way things work here. They work differently. I have important friends.'

Later that evening, Aijazul Haq drove me from Army House to Islamabad, past the airport which sits betwixt Rawalpindi and the modern capital. He was meeting President Ghulam Ishaq Khan. 'Just a courtesy call,' Aijazul winked as if to say he meant quite the opposite. 'GIK is one of our many friends.'

It did not take too long for Aijazul Haq to begin charting his promised comeback. He became a minister in Nawaz Sharif's first government and has since hung close to the centre of power in Islamabad. He fell out with Sharif when the Sharif-Ishaq Khan relationship soured but remained afloat in Islamabad. Aijazul retains strong links in two key movers of power in Pakistan that have often collaborated to kill democracy: the army and the Islamic fundamentalists. Who knows, Aijazul Haq may be the man Pervez Musharraf picks if he needs a civilian façade to broaden his regime's acceptance. He may yet be right about making a comeback. Who knows?

I went back to Peshawar. I wasn't supposed to return there but 'they', the popular Pakistani way of referring to the military establishment, changed my plans.

Hussain Haqqani, Nawaz Sharif's spruce spokesman, used to be a powerful man in Islamabad those days, or at least he liked to think he was. I met him at an arms dealer's soiree where, typically, the menu was gossip and Scotch, the ladies were perfumeries quaffing wine, the carpets Persian and the loos porcelain. The one I used had a lapis lazuli elephant the size of a St. Bernard and a musical toilet tissue holder. 'Once more, my love,' it intoned when the body had given all to the bidet.

Haqqani was holding forth to a fashionably attentive audience on the 'New Pakistan' emerging under Nawaz Sharif: democracy had dug deep roots, socioeconomic emancipation was underway — 'Look at the number of shopping plazas coming up in our cities' — and liberalism was gaining acceptance. Three cheers to Glenfiddich! I realised it was in my interest to give him room to expand on the theme. 'We are an open society, a confident, modern, democratic nation.... We are proving that to the world.....' I then suggested to him to let me visit Pakistani Kashmir. For all the room I had given him, Haqqani suddenly seemed wedged in a corner. But he was too savvy a party animal to stay stuck there long. 'Sure, sure,' he offered, 'no problem. We will arrange for you to go to "Azaad" Kashmir, you can see it for yourself.'

When I met Haqqani at the appointed hour in his office the next morning, he was singing another tune. 'The government would have been happy to send you to "Azaad" Kashmir, we have no problems, but they are not agreeing.'

'They?' I knew who, but I wanted Haqqani to spell it out.

'Well,' he said, 'between you and me the army says it will

not be possible to arrange such a trip at the moment. Why don't you go and see Mohenjo-Daro instead? We will be happy to arrange that.'

I said no, thank you, and went back to Peshawar.


The little boy began to fire in the air no sooner had we reached his shopfront. His body shook uncontrollably with the rat-a-tat of the gun; he was too young to absorb even the blunted recoil of a Kalashnikov. But he fired a whole round and then held out the weapon like a bouquet. 'Very good gun, Sir, easy to fire,' he said.

We were in Hayatabad, a hamlet in one of Pakistan's seven federally administered but hugely autonomous tribal agencies. It lay en route to Khyber Pass from Peshawar, close to the end of the Grand Trunk Road's run from Calcutta. My visa didn't allow me entry into tribal areas but Chacha said he had friends who would let us in without asking questions.

We had sped past the post manned by federal policemen, raising barely an eyebrow though many chutes of dust. 'We're there,' Chacha had said slowing the car down, 'in the land where there is no law but that of the gun. The government does not impose its will here, they leave everything to the tribesmen, even the law and its implementation.'

Hayatabad was just two columns of mud-and-timber shacks serried on either side of the road. Men, young and old, lounged on benches in the shopfronts, breathing dust. 'Kya chahiye, kya chahiye?' one of them called as we rolled by. 'Want to take a look?' Chacha asked me. We went inside the man's shack. It was a liquor parlour, unlit and bare. Plastic tumblers lay on planks arranged along wooden boxes they used for chairs. 'Anything you need, anything,' the man said as he ush-ered us into an anteroom. It was stacked with cratefuls of booze: a dozen premium brands of Scotch, white rum from Jamaica and South Africa, Napoleon brandy, Stolichnaya vodka, even locally bottled mao tai.

The walls were a rash of revolt against a society that imposes restrictions on overt interaction between the sexes: nudes and semi-nudes of the fairer form stuck with apparent lack of sophistry but alluring enough in themselves for the seeking client. Veils and billowing chadars (sheets) can starve you of the sight of a female face in and around Peshawar. Here, in this duty free shop of human indulgence, was room for release. Among members of the scanty collage were Helen and, for those who might still remember her, Faryal of the stretch pants and the slanted pout.

*Ganja, hashish, smack and speed were being sold with*
*stupefying openness in Hayatabad.*

Little kiosks, which at first looked like cigarette shops, sold narcotics with stupefying openness. Ganja, hashish, smack, speed, all neatly wrapped in cellophane and arranged by weight. Japanese refrigerators and air conditioners were piled in some shops like untended bricks. There were reams of Russian cotton, crockery from Oman and Iran, carpets from Central Asia. 'Cheap, Sir, and original. If you have problems with customs, we will ship it for you,' the storekeeper offered.

Contraband couriers were established business. You paid half the amount on purchase, half after delivery at your doorstep. The dealer took care of the courier's charges. Their profit margins must have been huge.

But the gunshops of Hayatabad were by far the most engaging. Any make, any vintage and they had it somewhere. If not in the shop, then in some storewell nearby. And given enough notice, they were ready to procure rocket launchers and hand-held anti-aircraft guns. That would only require a short expedition to Darra Adamkhel, the famed cottage industry of armaments whose artisans, through centuries of honing, could produce replicas of any weapon they laid their hands on. The story, perhaps apocryphal, was that in the late 1980s a team of arms experts from the US had gone up to Darra to have a look at their ways of working and the gun merchants offered them a deal: give us an F-16, they said, in return for as much land as you want in the Peshawar valley, and we shall make you a replica of it. The Americans declined, of course, but that is the kind of reputation Darra Adamkhel has.

'We have more guns,' the little Kalashnikov boy said, ducking into his shop, 'fresh from Darra. Chinese Kalashnikovs. More expensive but lighter and easier to fire.' I playfully asked him how I would take the gun out of the tribal agency, and he said, 'No problem. Everybody does it. The policemen will not check you, we are here.'

On the drive back, Chacha slipped a lapis lazuli lighter the shape of a revolver into my palm, a memento from Hayatabad. 'You could have got away with a real one, but this is absolutely safe to carry.' I lost it at Peshawar airport on the way out.

Before leaving Hayatabad, I asked the Kalashnikov boy's father, an old Afridi tribesman, how the vice vends he and his clansmen ran squared up with their puritanical faith. He rearranged the elaborate turban on his head, pawed his saucepan beard and said, 'Islam is dearest to us but we also have to live in order to follow it. The worldly and the ecclesiastical must coexist.'

There was another question troubling me about Hayatabad which I put to people in Islamabad on my return: Who needed Hayatabad? Why did these free-trade zones of malignance exist in Pakistan? The foreign minister, the portly Siddiq Kanju, offered an expected answer. 'They exist because they have been like this for ages. The tribals have their ways and we let them be.' A journalist friend said no politician in Pakistan would give a different answer. He explained things more truly and reasonably. 'Hayatabads exist because everybody needs them,' he said, 'They bring drug money and gun money. They supply alcohol for the glitterati. They supply guns and men to the militerati. Where do you think the Taliban come from? Their minds are conditioned in the Hayatabads of Pakistan, their guns are provided from there. Hayatabads are crucial to the powers that be in Pakistan.'

Successive governments have let the federally administered tribal agencies (FATAs) flourish because they have served their varied interests. Some, of course, have profited more from them than the others.

The maverick chief of the Jamaat-e-Islami, Maulana Fazlur Rehman, comes from a tribal agency like Hayatabad in the frontier province. In the past decade, Rehman has sprinkled Pakistan with deeni madrassas, religious training schools that breed the Taliban mindset and feed the mills of Islamic fundamentalism and militancy. But his original raising grounds for guns and jehadis (holy warriors) who wield those guns remain the FATAs.

Though he began electoral politics as a Nawaz Sharif ally in 1988, Rehman broke away in 1992 and endeared himself to the military establishment by rattling their favourite tunes: we need a more militant, more Islamic Pakistan, we need Kashmir from India at any cost. He never won a decent segment of the popular vote but what he could not achieve through politics, he always secured peddling the volatile fruits of Hayatabad: money, guns, men with guns, men opiated on Islam. Hayatabad is a laboratory men like Fazlur Rehman need to keep in business to sabotage experiments in democracy, few and fraudulent though they have been in Pakistan. Rehman was among the first to applaud when Musharraf snatched power.

Nawaz Sharif won a landslide victory in the elections of January 1997, an unprecedented two-thirds majority. But there was another message hidden in the mandate which made itself apparent only after his dismissal by General Musharraf: only thirty-five per cent voted in that election. So although Pakistanis were putting their faith in Nawaz Sharif, it was probably a last chance they were giving; their disenchantment with politicians was near the brim. No wonder no tears were shed when Sharif was bundled out.

But in January 1997, Sharif was still the toast of Pakistan. I missed the fireworks in Lahore — I was in the insulated refrigeration of Islamabad's winter, watching the fifth change of guard in Pakistan in a decade — but when I arrived two days later, Lahore was still celebrating. Shahid, whose taxi I hired at the airport, had a huge Nawaz poster emblazoned on the back seat. Sitting there, I had the strange feeling I had my arms around the prime minister's shoulders. But Shahid was a die-hard Nawaz fan even though he accused his men of cheating him. He had done some campaign trips for them and was owed Rs 5565 — he had the bill pasted on his dashboard — but they kept asking him to come later.

Shahid reminded me a bit of Chacha in the loving way he imposed himself on me. 'I'll drive you, till you are in Lahore, I'll drive you. Give me what you want.' He had a thing for Indians, he said, and my name had got him going about his favourite film *Sholay*. 'I must have seen it twenty times. So are you the *Sholay* kind of Thakur?' He did imitations of Gabbar Singh: 'Aao, Thakur, aao.' He was the kind of Pakistani that can easily give you the silly idea that they want to be one nation with India. He loved aspects of India like its films and music, as most Pakistanis do, but he was a proud Pakistani, as most Pakistanis are. 'I love Ameeta Bachchan and your Madhuri Dixit but I don't like what you do in Kashmir. And when you beat us in cricket, that is the thing I dislike most.'

That night Shahid took me to what he called a *Sholay* kind of place — to Bundu Khan's open-air eatery near Lahore's Fortress Stadium. The *Sholay* bit was whole lambs skewered and roasting over a massive circular pit. 'Very exclusive place,' Shahid said, 'top army people come here.' Nothing better to recommend a place in Pakistan.

It was a cold, dewey night and it was warm around the glow of the pit. The air was festive — a new government, a new beginning, the leftover fireworks were still bursting in Lahore's skies in ones and twos. Bundu Khan's was playing a live recording of Iqbal Bano singing Faiz Ahmed Faiz, songs of repression and rebellion. '*Hum dekhenge, hum dekhenge, Jab takht giraye jaayenge aur taj uchhale jaayenge, hum dekhenge…*' (We shall see, we shall see… the day the thrones are razed and the crowns are tossed away…we shall see, we shall see.) Shahid took me to a shop in the Fortress Stadium where I bought Iqbal Bano's music and some more songs of Faiz by Nayyara Noor.

We stayed out late. On the way back to the hotel, Shahid subconsciously hummed the Faiz song. An election had just been held, the army had been out of power for close to a decade, but Faiz's poetry of freedom lost and freedom regained still strummed a chord in Pakistan, as if the nation remained afraid of losing what it had and longed still for what it had not.

Shahid wasn't coming the next day. It would be 5 February, Kashmir Day in Pakistan. Not safe on the streets for Indians, he said, and not safe to be with Indians. He was frank enough. He took a break. I ventured out on my own mid-morning. Anarkali Bazaar was drowned in a normal day's bustle. Along the adjacent Lahore Mall, now called the Shara-e-Quaid-e-Azam, about twenty demonstrators were staging a protest: black flags, blue breasts, blazing slogans: *Kashmir mein Katl-e-aam band karo, band karo! Kashmir hamara wapas do, wapas do! India hai, hai! India hai hai!*

Nobody paid much attention. I bought several pairs of socks from a street-corner stall as I watched the procession pass. 'Guaranteed to last,' the salesman said. They were soft and fawn.

The salesman was right. They did last. They are still often on my feet, as cuddly and as soft, though not as fawn. Pakistan, meanwhile, has slid back under the jackboot.

# Talking With the Enemy'

## MANI SHANKAR AIYAR

India's former consul-general in Karachi on why India must keep talking to Pakistan and why India's traditional distaste for the Pakistan military is not borne out by the record.

As the consul-general of India, I was at Karachi airport on the night of 3 April 1979, annoyed because the ranking Pakistani general was not there to receive General Malhotra, chief of the Indian army staff, who was transiting through Karachi on his way back to Delhi from an official visit to Kenya. Next morning I learned the reason for this breach of protocol. The ranking general was busy getting the grave dug at Rato Dero in upper Sindh to receive the body of Zulfiqar Ali Bhutto, who was hanged that night in his jail at Rawalpindi a few hours after our man had taken off for Delhi.

Karachi, like all of Pakistan, received the news in stunned silence and queasy calm. There were no demonstrations, no great sign of public mourning. The writer Khushwant Singh was on a visit to Islamabad. He was my writer-wife's patron saint and father of one of my school-cum-college friends. He rang from the capital in high excitement. What's happening? When is the revolution spilling into the streets? Nothing is happening, I replied, all is eerily normal, people are going about their work as usual, nothing is closed, nothing is being shut down.

'I'm getting into Karachi on Friday morning right on time for the *jumma* prayers,' he said. 'That is when the protests will begin.' I shrugged my shoulders. A shrug cannot be conveyed on the telephone. I escorted Uncle Khushwant into the VIP lounge the minute his flight landed. He asked me to drive him around the city, instead of going straight home. Nothing stimulates a journalist so much as the prospect of being an eye-witness to history. But it was not Uncle Khushwant's moment. Nothing was happening. The streets were becalmed, the stores closed for the weekly holiday, the populace indoors (doubtless hoping that, if their luck held, the ether waves would bring

**203**

them the afternoon Hindi movie from the Muscat TV channel).We drove past the Bagh-e-Jinnah. There was a group of schoolboys playing cricket in the spring sun. That was when Uncle Khushwant lost heart. 'Let's go home,' he said.

Once home, I told him the story of our tailor. We were doing up Hindusthan Court, abandoned since the 1965 war, and being restored after thirteen long years on our post being re-opened with my arrival in Karachi in December 1978. The country was agog with the Bhutto trial. Days after I got in, the Lahore high court held Bhutto guilty and sentenced him to hang by the neck till dead. The appeal was taken swiftly to the Supreme Court. Bhutto appeared in person before the bench, declared his innocence and his faith in the impartiality of the judiciary, and received in return the Supreme Court's confirmation of the death sentence.

It was a majority judgement, not a unanimous decision. This wedged the door open to a deluge of demands for mercy. Virtually every foreign office in the world called in Pakistani diplomats to present demarches for Bhutto to be saved from the gallows. The Pakistani dictator sneered at these cry-baby claims, dismissing them, in a telling phrase, as being raised by 'a trade union of politicians.' The Indian government was conspicuous by the tight-lipped silence it alone maintained. No request was made for clemency. The Indian external affairs minister was one Atal Behari Vajpayee.

As the drama unfolded, I asked the Pakistani tailor who was doing our curtains for Hindusthan Court what would happen if Bhutto were, in fact, hanged. 'Rivers of blood,' he intoned with passion, 'will flow in the streets of the city.' (The words sounded even more impassioned in the original Urdu.) I asked him whether he was a supporter of Bhutto's PPP (Pakistan People's

Party). 'Don't you see this?' he replied, pointing to the golf cap on his head. It was the emblem made notorious by Bhutto when he wore it to the Martyrs' Memorial in Dhaka, erected to the hundreds of thousands of East Pakistanis gunned down by the Pakistani Army because Bhutto would not let Sheikh Mujibur Rahman assume office as prime minister after he had trounced the PPP in the first truly democratic election held in Pakistan. I had run into the tailor again the morning after the hanging. Why, I had asked him, were the streets of Karachi not running with rivers of blood? Infinitely sad, heartbroken, the tailor said, 'Because our leaders have let us down.' Then, said I, why are you still wearing your PPP golf cap? 'No one,' he replied wearily, 'has ordered me to take it off. If they do, I will.'

That was when I knew I was right in what till then, flying in the face of conventional wisdom, I had only guessed at: that Zia was in for keeps and nothing would remove him but the Angel of Death. Our embassy in Islamabad, of course, spent all its time drafting coded despatches to Delhi about how the revolution was just round the corner, a matter of months and that the people would rise to string up the hated Zia. In the event, Zia, like Tennyson's brook, went on and on. It took a good eleven years after his coup d'etat for Zia to meet his end in an as yet unexplained air crash. Chances are the crash was probably engineered by Shia clerics who regarded Zia's near-Wahabi version of Sunni-ization as dangerously un-Islamic.

Distaste for the Pakistan military has been the leitmotif of India's Pakistan policy ever since Ayub Khan's military takeover in October 1958. Yet, the record, if carefully examined, does not bear out our traditional distrust of the Pakistani brass and our corresponding, if despairing, faith in Pakistan's civil political establishment. It is not that military governments have been better for us than civil governments, but that they have been no worse. The army is the most pervasive, powerful, permanent political party in Pakistan. Whether the political establishment wears a civilian mask or bares its military teeth, it is the army which ultimately calls the shots. Talking to the civilian authority in Pakistan is, therefore, a bit like talking to V. George; talking directly to the armed forces is more the *asli cheez*. Hence the importance of assessing the nature and consequences of Gen. Pervez Musharraf's ascension to overt political authority in the mirror of India's previous experience of dealing with Pakistan under presidents in uniform compared to Pakistan under prime ministers in mufti.

It was the civilian government of the Quaid-e-Azam, Mohammed Ali Jinnah, which ordered the raid into Kashmir in October 1947, followed by the regular war which took up much of 1948. It was again at the instigation of a civilian politician, foreign minister Zulfiqar Ali Bhutto, that the lunge towards Akhnur was launched in September 1965. Air Marshal Asghar Khan's *The First Round* reveals that as Pakistan's long-serving chief of air staff, he had no knowledge of, nor were any preparations made by the defence forces, for taking on India in the battlefield, at least till the air marshal's retirement in July 1965. There followed the next month — August 1965 — the fiasco of the Bhutto-inspired Operation Gibraltar. The infiltrated militants failed to foster an uprising in the Valley and were rounded up, almost to a man, on intelligence provided to India by local Kashmiris.

That led to Bhutto holding a highly secret, unrecorded and unconfirmed one-on-one tete-a-tete with Chinese Premier

Chou en-Lai at Karachi airport. Although no one has been able to ascertain the veracity of the claim, since no one else was present and Chou en-Lai never confirmed or denied what was attributed to him, Bhutto asserted in Cabinet that Chou had assured him the Chinese pincer would move into India in the northeast as soon as the Pakistani pincer moved into the north-west. Bhutto was taken at his word. The international border was crossed. But the Chinese pincer never materialised.

Beyond complaining that Indian jawans had stolen thirty-two of their sheep (which led to Indian demonstrators attempting to drive thirty-two sheep into the Chinese embassy compound in Chanakyapuri, New Delhi), there was no matching military action by China to the Pakistani move. Meanwhile, appalled that Pakistan had fulfilled the Indian prediction of arms supplied by the Western powers for fighting the Soviet Union being used in aggression against India, the US and British envoys informed the Pakistan government that military supplies were being immediately cut off. And Field Marshal Ayub Khan, who had earlier talked of leading his troops into battle, locked himself up in his Rawalpindi den, terrified of what would become of him.

The war over, Bhutto did a neat about turn accusing the generals, in the manner of Corporal Hitler, of having betrayed the jawan. Bhutto was dismissed. And that led eventually to the ouster of Ayub. Meanwhile, Bhutto founded his PPP and Ayub's place was taken by his chosen successor, Gen. Yahya Khan. Yahya organised the first genuine democratic election in Pakistan, but then helplessly obeyed orders when the defeated candidate, Zulfiqar Ali Bhutto, insisted on a genocidal crackdown in the east. That ended in yet another civilian-fostered war with India.

We have now had Kargil, the latest in the long line of wars foisted on India by an elected, civilian authority in Pakistan. To cover up the fact of Nawaz Sharif having taken Vajpayee quite literally for a ride, the Vajpayee government put up George Fernandes to argue the wholly bogus point that Sharif was unaware of what his army was up to. Brajesh Mishra, the prime minister's principal secretary, and External Affairs Minister Jaswant Singh sought to make the same point. However, neither Nawaz Sharif nor any of his civilian cohorts has disavowed their military's action; how could they? They were up to their necks in the conspiracy to cross the LoC and interdict supplies to Siachen. They must have been amazed at the naivete of Vajpayee clambering on to a bus for Lahore at the same time as Pakistani jawans and terrorists were clambering on to buses headed for the LoC. Alternatively, Sharif must have assumed that the Indian prime minister was in the know of what was known to Indian intelligence (as now confirmed by the Subrahmanyam Committee of Inquiry) that Pakistan was readying for its most massive thrust ever. If, nonetheless, Vajpayee was prepared to play the Sharif game of waging war and peace at the same time, Sharif was delighted to play along. What Sharif could not have assumed was the Vajpayee government's criminal neglect of raw intelligence which the Pakistanis must have assumed would be in the hands of the Indian government. Yes, Kargil was Musharraf's war, but no less was it Sharif's.

In addition to the military record of Pakistan's civilian governments, it would also be instructive to examine the civilian record of their military governments. I begin with the insights of Rajeshwar Dayal, the Indian high commissioner appointed on the eve of Ayub Khan's October 1958 coup. Dayal visited Pakistan on behalf of the Aga Khan Foundation while I was in Karachi. He told me of how, in the early 1940s, when he was district magistrate in Mathura, Ayub's brother was his superintendent of police. Ayub himself was posted in nearby Agra and would often drive up for a convivial evening. In 1958, when Dayal went to Karachi, which was then the capital of Pakistan, Ayub came round for a strictly private conversation. He told Dayal that the two of them had six months to do whatever they could to sort out Indo-Pak relations; 'thereafter,' said Ayub, 'the politicians will hold me in hock.'

Ayub Khan supervised the compromises that led to the Indus Waters Agreement, which has lasted to this day, engendering the Green Revolution in both Indian and Pakistani Punjab. It is that agreement which has made South Asia, stalking home of famine, self-sufficient in food.

The other outcome of Ayub's military takeover, according to Dayal, might have been the 'Trieste solution' to the question of Kashmir. Trieste and its surroundings are claimed by both Italy and Austria. Italy is in physical possession; Austria has not renounced its claim. But both countries, recognising the complexities of their conflicting claims and the impossibility of reconciling these, have agreed that the claims of both countries might be kept alive *de jure* but, for the nonce, the status quo would prevail *de facto*. The dispute would be resolved, if ever, at an indefinite date in the future when it might prove possible to do so.

Following the Indus Waters Treaty, Jawaharlal Nehru embarked on an extended tour of Pakistan. Kuldip Nayar's *Distant Neighbours* graphically recounts the disaster. Nehru wanted to address a public meeting in Karachi. Instead, he was subjected to a civic reception (which meant the public were kept out and the invitation list was restricted to *burra sahibs* — feudal lords, ICS *koi-hai*s and Blimpish colonels dressed in dinner jackets and cummerbunds!) Protests from the Indian side led to a public meeting being arranged eventually, but with exquisite indelicacy, in the bazaar at Murree, venue of the first massacre of the Sikhs in the orgy of mutual violence that accompanied the Great British Scuttle, otherwise known as the Partition of India.

To make up, Ayub invited Nehru to drive together from Murree to Ayub's home-town of Abbotabad. But the fastidious democrat in Panditji could not bear the thought of having to make small talk with a military dictator. Not a word was exchanged between them as they drove down to Nathiagali. Insulted, Ayub withdrew to his own car, the rest of the journey being completed in mutual disdain. Not quite the atmosphere for a Trieste solution to the problem of Kashmir.

*Z*ia took over in July 1977 as the next military dictator after Yahya, following a brief allegedly 'democratic' interregnum under Bhutto (1971-77). Zia went overboard with overtures to India, all unreciprocated, especially after the Morarji government, which had held its tongue over the Bhutto hanging, fell within three months of the judicial assassination. Zia's ambassador in Delhi, Abdus Sattar, now foreign minister to 'Chief Executive' Musharraf, was hated by the establishment but toasted by the *aam janata*. Not since Raja Ghaznafar Ali Khan in the mid-fifties had a Pakistani diplomat been such a hit with the Delhi party crowd. Sattar's command performance was in keeping with Zia's concept of foreign policy as public relations: give nothing away of substance but never let the smile on your face wear thin. (That Sattar's was a command performance was established by his surly retreat when briefly posted again to Delhi in the early 1990s.)

Zia played up his Stephanian connection as the key to informal diplomacy. His reverence for his old history teacher, the aging E.R. Kapadia, was ostentatiously put on display, a team of young Stephanians under Professor Kapadia's charge being invited as guests of the government to Pakistan. That paved the way for Zia to get himself invited to his alma mater (whose most distinguished alumnus he was) in its centenary year (1981). The public face of his PR meshed with its private face. I was witness to a revealing instance of this. A young Stephanian squash player came to play the renowned Pakistani team at a tournament in Karachi. His father had been Zia's senior in the same regiment of the pre-Partition Indian Army. Following the end of the tournament, there was a banquet. The team and I were part of the queue that formed to bid the president farewell as he left the banquet. Zia passed us with his usual fixed smile attached to his moustache. A few yards down, he returned to take his friend's son to one side. They conversed a few minutes. Zia left. The boy returned to where we were, his expression both beatific and bemused. We asked what the president had said. 'He said, when you go home please tell your mother that in Pakistan you met Zia ul-Haq. I think she will remember me.'

Artful PR or disarming humility? Who knows? There was no visiting Indian journalist, howsoever humble, who did not find a ready place at Zia's table. A flurry of Pakistani artistes visited India — to hysterical applause from appreciative audiences. I restored our auditorium in Karachi and arranged for several Indian artistes to come, including a delegation of Gujarati poets (it is little remembered in most of India that Gujarati is Karachi's second language). More important, I opened our auditorium to Pakistani artistes. Every Indo-Pak event, of whatever little significance, was celebrated, including the defeat of India by a Pakistani bridge team. The local press could not get over India House congratulating the Pakistan victors before the Pakistan government got around to doing so; less surprisingly, perhaps, in Zia's puritanical Pakistan, it was the Indian consulate-general that organised a congratulatory evening for Nazia Hassan singing the smash hit *Aap jaisa koi*, the first Indo-Pak joint venture in pop music since Partition.

There was goodwill in the air but no progress at all on the political front. Vajpayee's March 1978 visit to Pakistan — the first by an Indian foreign minister since Nehru's death in 1964 — set bells ringing, but the Morarji government fell before anything could come of it. Indira Gandhi's Second Coming in 1980 more or less coincided with the Soviet invasion of Afghanistan and the consequent teaming up of the US with Pakistan. Foreign Secretary Ram Sathe came visiting, followed by External Affairs Minister P.V.Narasimha Rao, but the glacier was not moving. It was not till the end of January 1982, under a month of my transfer to Delhi, that the first slight signs of a thaw set in.

Veteran Pakistan Foreign Minister Agha Shahi led a team which arrived in time for the traditional Beating Retreat ceremony on 29 January which marks the end of the Republic Day celebrations. Narasimha Rao gathered the Indian delegation together after the welcome reception in Hyderabad House to ask the most pertinent question, 'Why is he here?' The others had their say. I hazarded the hypothesis that while Zia had secured his authority in Pakistan, he lacked both legitimacy and popularity in the eyes of his people. Short of restoring democracy to his country, which would, of course, end his authority — and probably his life — the only way the Pakistan president could win legitimacy and acceptance in Pakistan would be to demonstrate that he had it in him to engage India in a meaningful dialogue. I advised that we take the visit seriously as an earnest desire to move forward on various bilateral matters, if not on Kashmir, Afghanistan or Pak support to 'Khalistan' militants.

The Agha Shahi visit was one of the temporary highs in Indo-Pak relations; it took no more than an argument in the UN Human Rights Commission the following month for the setback to set in. Yet, however much Zia remained involved in fomenting his proxy war in Punjab (and readying for the same in Kashmir), there was an impressive persistence to the way he kept returning to India and seeking out the Indian prime minister at gatherings in South Asia and overseas (funerals, summits and so forth). At least one major crisis was defused by his insistent courtesy and disregard for protocol.

While Prime Minister Rajiv Gandhi was away in the Andaman and Nicobar islands from the last week of December 1986 to the first week of January 1987, India and Pakistan moved to the brink of war. The proximate cause was Pakistani alarm at the preparations being made for the most overwhelming military exercise ever undertaken by India, Operation Brasstacks. Nervous that this was no military exercise but a preparation for the real thing, the Pakistani armed forces started mobilising and moving out of peace-time stations towards the frontier. In turn, the Indian armed forces began readying for the contingency of the exercise turning into war. It was while the prime minister was away that the eyeball-to-eyeball confrontation reached its most dangerous pitch.

Neither his minister of state for defence, Arun Singh, nor his chief of army staff, Gen. K. Sundarji, kept their prime minister informed of the gravity of the military crisis. They were too tied up playing their personal war game — with real soldiers, not wooden toys. My duties in the Prime Minister's Office (where I was serving on deputation from the foreign office as a joint secretary) were not such that I would normally have got wind of what was happening. But Rajiv was well-acquainted with my Pakistan connection. He had also laughed when, at the start of the Pakistan president's courtesy call on the Indian prime minister at Muscat in November 1985, on being asked by Zia, 'How are you?' I had replied, 'Still on your side, Sir!'

Perhaps because of this background, Rajiv Gandhi called me on the RAX one morning, as the crisis was beginning to come off the boil, to ask whether I thought a summit encounter might be possible and, if so, how best it might be arranged. I told him the best option from our point of view would be to invite Zia to Delhi for a luncheon meeting at which just the two of them could get together and confirm ways of defusing the crisis and keeping it defused. I added, however, that as Zia had already come to India half-a-dozen times without his visits being reciprocated, there was the protocol problem of how he could come once again and that too when the two countries were on the threshold of armed hostilities. I, therefore, sugges-ted four other options in descending order of preference: Zia being invited not to the capital, Delhi, but to, say, Amritsar; our prime minister going to Lahore, but not to Islamabad; or, if that failed, our prime minister making a quick no-frills working visit to the Pakistan capital; and, finally, counsel of despair, meeting in a third country.

I am not privy to who the others consulted were and what their advice was. Nor am I privy to what Rajiv told Zia on the hot line. What is in public knowledge is that Zia promptly came over to Delhi, spent no more than a few hours over lunch at Hyderabad House in a strictly one-on-one encounter, and left immediately thereafter. The crisis ended.

Several months later, the prime minister asked me to sound out the Pakistan high commissioner, the always affable Humayun Khan. When I paid Humayun a slightly undercover visit, the high commissioner read out to me Zia's handwritten

*Zia and Rajiv met in a strictly one-on-one encounter in New Delhi in 1987 and defused a war crisis.*

record of his conversation with Rajiv Gandhi. If Zia had not made it to president, he would have made a great foreign service third secretary, so precisely and meticulously was the record written from memory immediately after the meeting.

Eighteen months later, Zia was dead. His eleven years as president were a period of great tension in Indo-Pak relations, beginning with public revulsion over his judicial assassination of Bhutto (however solicitous of Zia's sensitivities the Morarji-Vajpayee government might have been), going on to the imbroglio engendered by the Soviet incursion into Afghanistan, followed by Zia's outrageous support to the 'Khalistan' militants, the outbreak of hostilities in Siachen, repeated alarums over our military exercises, the stoking of the Kashmir issue at the UN, and the first confirmation of Pakistan having a basement nuclear bomb. Besides, there were tensions over communal incidents in India, especially after the riots which followed the firing at the Eidgah in Moradabad on the very day of the solemn festival of Eid. Meanwhile, every forward movement on bilateral relations turned out to be a false start. Yet, the sheer persistence of Zia's efforts at keeping the door open to dialogue so ameliorated the atmosphere that no one lost any real sleep over Pakistan going to war with India.

The contrast with the eleven years of civilian rule (1988-99) that followed Zia's air crash needs to be noted.

Benazir Bhutto was born in 1953, Rajiv Gandhi in 1943, both Midnight's Children. There was a sentimental but high hope that, free of the hang-ups of the generation that had endured the horrors of Partition, there could be the breaking

*Benazir failed to honour an agreement on Siachen reached between her and Rajiv in 1989.*

of a new dawn under these two young leaders. Rajiv Gandhi gave voice to this hope in an unusual banquet speech in July 1989, on his second visit in a year to Islamabad: 'When our two countries attained independence, I was a child, almost an infant, and you, Madam Prime Minister, were yet to be born. You and I have grown, as the vast majority of our peoples have grown, in a world in which India, as she is now, and Pakistan, as a sovereign, independent entity, are established realities. It falls upon our generation to safeguard our sovereignties not through the illusory pursuit of military strength but through the conscious pursuit of friendship among ourselves. It falls upon us to silence the guns that have given no peace and to seek the enduring solutions that only peaceful coexistence can ensure.'

Alas, the grape withered on the vine.

Benazir failed to rise to the occasion. An agreement was reached between them on Siachen, relating to demarcating the LoC through the glacier, but it was not formally promoted by her or even openly acknowledged. She sent a wholly apolitical hotelier, 'Happy' Minwalla (chosen because he was a Parsi like Rajiv's father?) to explain to Rajiv that she was not able to sell the accord to her army. Once Rajiv lost the election of November 1989 and the successor V.P. Singh government freed a number of terrorists to secure the release of his home minister, Mufti Mohammad Sayeed's kidnapped daughter, Rubaiya, Benazir could not resist the temptation of fishing in the troubled waters of cross-border terrorism. The proxy war in Kashmir was her war, even as the wars of 1965 and 1971 were her father's wars.

She also missed out on another opportunity furnished her by the Narasimha Rao government when, on her once again becoming prime minister in October 1993, Rao sent her a congratulatory letter in which, for the first time ever, India offered to engage in talks with Pakistan on 'issues related to Jammu & Kashmir.' Foreign Secretary J.N.Dixit's *My South Block Years* reveals, partly by what it says but mostly by what it does not (e.g. no reference at all to the congratulatory letter), how nothing came of the offer: neither side was really serious or sincere about a diplomatic initiative to determinedly address the problem. Out of power, Benazir has had the grace and intelligence to herself admit that her biggest mistake was her hawkishness over Kashmir. It was such hawkishness that marked both her tenures, 1988-90 and 1993-96. The two countries teetered on the brink of war, with no progress over any matter and none of the whiffs of goodwill so characteristic of the Zia era.

The elections in Pakistan in February 1997 sparked a new round of hope. I was in Pakistan to write on the significance of the outcome for *India Today*. Nawaz Sharif gave me my theme by making good relations with India the main plank of his platform in the final phase of the campaign. I argued that the Pakistani budget just could not continue carrying the burden of the current level of defence expenditure without rendering the economy bankrupt; at the same time, there was no way defence expenditure could be cut without its being demonstrated that an India-Pakistan dialogue was really underway. I concluded that this was an opportunity we must not miss. Moreover, on our side of the border, the external affairs minister was that Pakistani favourite, Inder Kumar Gujral, shortly destined to become prime minister. The prospect seemed pregnant with possibilities.

Another false dawn. Neither Sharif's democratically secured two-thirds majority nor all of Gujral's *mushairas* and *mehfils* led to a new spring. Gujral let himself be caught in a procedural wrangle over the forum at which the issue of Jammu & Kashmir was to be discussed. The Pakistanis had one interpretation of what the two foreign secretaries had agreed to in Murree in June 1997; we another. The fact that the argument was later resolved only showed how poorly prepared were the preparations for the dialogue. Talks about talks are the essential pre-requisite to substantive dialogue. The way to substantive dialogue has never been properly smoothed, and this in itself has contributed to the repeated breakdown of the dialogue.

Dialogue turned to deception after Vajpayee replaced Gujral as prime minister. Whatever Nawaz Sharif's apologists might say — and they range from George Fernandes and

Brajesh Mishra to the hopelessly outwitted Jaswant Singh and Vajpayee — democracy and civil rule in Pakistan duped India in 1999 as India has never before been duped. At the very instant that Vajpayee was readying himself for his much-hyped but essentially ridiculous bus to Pakistan, his host (and the guns at the host's temple) were readying for Kargil.

The man who held that gun is now the boss in Pakistan, with the curious title of chief executive. Do we deal with him?

Do we have an alternative? Ayub lasted eleven years; Zia lasted eleven. 'Democracy' lasted eleven. Perhaps then the numerological assumption to make would be that Musharraf will last his eleven! The fact is the strongest political party in Pakistan is the army. Sometimes it runs the government itself. At others, it lends outside support to the civilian authority. But any Pakistani politician who backs the army is only storing up his own dismissal. Pakistan will go democratic only if it merges into India. That will not happen. Ergo, Pakistan's only destiny is to remain a protectorate of its own armed forces.

It is this reality we have to deal with. It is this reality we balk at recognising. There is first our distaste of dealing with dictators. This, however, is a somewhat selective distaste as many of our best friends have been, and are, dictators. We seem to become squeamish only when dealing with Pakistani dictators. Then there is our solicitousness for the people of Pakistan. The politicians of Pakistan are the first to squawk when an Ayub or a Yahya, a Zia or a Musharraf takes over. But when given a shot at running the system, civilian rule in Pakistan quickly degenerates into feudal rule and coterie rule.

The only Pakistani, of the thousands I met in Karachi, who openly supported Zia explained it to me thus: 'All these guys who complain are cosily linked to each other. So, whoever rules, their personal or business work gets done. Zia is the first outsider. They don't know how to break into his circle. That is why they hate him.'

Indian democracy, for all its faults, is a working democracy because land reforms and swinging socialism have together empowered a middle class which competes for the franchise of the poor. In Pakistan, there has been no land reform, no socialism, plenty of monopoly capital and, therefore, a 'democracy' in which the rich rotate until the armed forces stop the roundabout and start riding themselves.


The other argument against dealing with Pakistani military dictators is that they are Islamists. That, of course, was not true of Ayub or of the fun-loving Yahya, but has become the stereotypical image of Pakistani military dictators after the pious Zia. I have never quite understood how the Islamisation of Pakistan constitutes a danger to us. Do Indian Muslims regard Pakistani Muslims as their role models? Ausaf Vasfi, the editor of *Radiance*, the organ of the Jamaat-e-Islami of India, slipped into a press conference of Zia's and berated the Pakistan president for the utterly un-Islamic condition of Pakistan under the Nizam-e-Mustafa (The Rule of Allah). It was one of the most sensational media events of my time. Partition is half a century behind us. The Pakistani pretension to being the voice of the Muslims of the subcontinent stands punctured. The Indian Muslim is finding his destiny in India. Pakistan is for him no exemplar.

Had Partition never taken place, or if Partition had been so arranged that a large non-Muslim minority remained in (West) Pakistan, there might have been some slight hope of Pakistan going the secular way, as Jinnah appears to have hoped, going by his much-quoted address to the Pakistan Constituent Assembly on 11 August 1947. But once Pakistan emerged as a virtually cent per cent Muslim country, it was inevitable that it would then emerge as an Islamic state.

I was in Pakistan when Zia declared the Nizam-e-Mustafa on the first of Rabi-ul-Awwal, 4 February 1979. The Karachi Boat Club (best lobsters and crabs in the subcontinent) hailed its advent by decorating the bar in black. Bhutto had banned Muslims from drinking in public places. The Nizam-e-Mustafa meant I could not buy them a drink. There were uninformed policemen who thought Zia actually meant it. So, they raided Amy Haque's house and ferreted out a few forgotten bottles. As the wife of a Pakistan test cricketer and a relative of Begum Para, the smash-hit film star of Zia's youth, Amy was no nobody. So, Zia added a coda to his Nizam-e-Mustafa, viz., that a Pakistani's home is his castle and so the police are not allowed to raid anyone to see whether he has cached away a bit of the bubbly.

In consequence, when Foreign Secretary Ram Sathe asked me what qualities he should look for in finding my successor, I replied, 'A strong liver.' The Nizam-e-Mustafa, at least south of the aforementioned 'Happy' Minwalla's Metropole Hotel, floated on a sea of alcohol. Those who never drank (some ninety-five per cent of the populace) were patted on the back by Zia's Islamisation, and those who liked their tipple were left to get on with their tributes to Scotland. One prominent Pakistani politician, who went on to become PM for a few months, defined Zia's oppression to me in the following words (I swear!): 'Before the bastard took over, I used to have twenty-four brands of whisky in my house. Now, I'm down to six.'

More seriously, the problem in Pakistan is not whether to be Islamic but what 'Islamic' means. Omar Khayyam, eight centuries ago, warned that the 'two and seventy jarring sects confute'; in Pakistan, criminal law is having difficulty basing itself on the Shariat since the Fiqah Hanafi of the Sunnis says the hand begins at the wrist while the Fiqah Jafaria of the Shias says the bit to cut off begins at the fingers. Both are the Word of God; therefore, irrefutable and also irreconcilable. So, for petty larceny, no thief (at least while I was there) lost his 'hand' (howsoever defined).

Islam is what unites Pakistan; Islamisation is what divides it. Which is why Zia was killed not by a secular alcoholic but by a group of enraged Shia clerics.

Moreover, there is another Pakistan, the Pakistan of Shiva-ratri on Clifton Beach in Karachi where Hindu worshippers (mostly scheduled castes) snake their way into a cavernous *gupha*, at the far end of which is one of the most impressive natural *lingam*s to be seen anywhere on the subcontinent. Diwali cards are put on the market for sale every October. The president of the Pak-Hind Prem Sabha (a Pakistani Muslim) is unfailing in sending me Diwali greetings every year.

I was introduced to this other Pakistan the day I arrived there. The district magistrate of Sukkur called me to ask a favour. A Hindu *sant* from India was visiting Hayat Pitafi after a gap of several years; his Muslim *mureeds* wanted to seek the *sant*'s blessings. Would India have any objection? No, I said rather grandly (and a bit smugly, if truth be told!), none at all.

Later, when I had become close friends with Amin Fahim, the eldest son of the Pir of Hala (and now himself the Pir) I made bold to ask him whether his father had Hindu followers. 'Of course,' said the Pir-designate, 'and they still seek our blessings, even from India, when there is a birth in the family, or a wedding or the son gets a job.' Presuming on our friendship, I allowed myself to ask whether it was not true that the blessings of the Pir had to be validated by the payment of a *nazrana*. Yes, he confirmed, *nazrana* has to be paid, even as little as five or ten rupees but it has to be paid. Then, I asked, how do these Indian Hindu *bhakta*s send their *nazrana*? Fahim found the answer laughingly obvious. 'Through the smugglers, of course,' he said, 'that's how the requests for blessings come and that's how my father sends them his benediction.'

The twist now being given to the earlier argument about Islam in Pakistan being a threat to India is the Taliban connections of Pervez Musharraf. I find this a curious argument. The Taliban is a creation of Pakistan. It is not the cause of Pakistani hostility. Moreover, the Taliban is preoccupied with consolidating its hold over Afghanistan and fighting off the counter-claims of other Muslim factions in Afghanistan. The Taliban government's relations with Pakistan are uneasy and all the problems that, for half a century, have bedevilled Afghanistan-Pakistan relations (notably, the non-acceptance by Afghanistan of the Durrand Line that divides Pushto-speaking areas of Afghanistan from Pushto-speaking areas of Pakistan) remain unresolved. True, there are Taliban militants in the Kashmir Valley. They are, however, an adjunct to the Pakistan armed forces, not a substitute. This the Pakistanis discovered to their cost in Kargil last year when their pretence that the LoC had been crossed not by Pakistan army regulars but inflamed religious fanatics found no takers. There is little harm the Taliban can do us in Kashmir except at the behest of, and in concert with, Pakistan. Our problem is the general himself, not his cross-border connections in Afghanistan. If the Taliban had not existed, our problem with Pakistan would still remain.

Another fantasy much put about is of Islamic fanatics taking over Pakistan and then declaring *jehad* on India. It is a fantasy which unites the 'clash of civilisations' types of the Western world with the communal mindset of the sangh parivar. The Pakistanis are Muslims, not mad mullahs. The Jamaat-e-Islami, for instance, has never been able to win more than a single seat to the Pakistan national assembly. Osama Bin Laden or the Lashkar-e-Toeba would first have to conquer Pakistan before turning to India. Conquering Pakistan they cannot do, not only because everything that is modern-minded, cultured and reasonable in Pakistan would oppose it, but because the Pakistani Army would not stand for it. The Pakistani Army has become the single most influential political element in Pakistan because of its stringent discipline. The symbol of that army is a Pervez Musharraf who holds dogs in his hands and gets himself photographed with his wife outside of a *burqa*.

Our problem is not the religious colour of our Pakistani counterparts but their nationalistic hostility to India as a nation. That hostility has its causes, reasonable and unreasonable. It finds expression in defining the identity of Pakistan not

*The symbol of the Pakistani Army is not a fundamentalist but a Pervez Musharraf who gets himself photographed with his wife outside of a burqa.*

in terms of Pakistan's own nationhood but in contradistinction to the nationhood of India. The challenge before India lies in responding to these deep-running causes in a rational manner, not in spinning out nightmares of Pakistan's Islamic hordes joining hands with India's Islamic hordes to do down Hindu India. Our opponent is Pervez Musharraf, not Mahmoud of Ghazni.

The final argument against dealing with a Pakistan crushed under the cruel heel of its army is that the armed forces are bent on avenging themselves for Bangladesh. The argument always brings to mind my first evening out in Karachi. I asked the gentleman seated next to me the subcontinental equivalent of conversing about the weather.

'Have you been to India?' I said.

'Yes,' he answered.

'Where did you go?'

'Meerut,' he replied.

'Oh really, and how long were you there?'

'Two-and-a-half years,' he said.

It slowly dawned on me why. Embarrassed, I started stammering my apologies. 'Yes, yes, I was your prisoner-of-war. And tell me can you join me at the Sindh Club tomorrow evening at eight? They've got an excellent port laid down, which we can all finish together.'

He and his wife remain, after twenty years, among my closest friends in Karachi.

Yes, there is a problem of revenge. It is not a sentiment exclusive to the armed forces. Given half a chance, any red-blooded Pakistani would do what he can to harm us. But we have to give him the opening. He troubles us in Punjab when Punjab goes up in flames. He troubles us in Kashmir when we cannot contain violence in the Valley. He infiltrates Assam when he sees we are with a problem there. And he hijacks our planes to get out our terrorists (who are his 'freedom fighters'). Getting Pakistan targeted as a 'terrorist state' is a sound weapon of war in this battle of diplomatic attrition. But it is not a solution to our problems.

Pakistan is both a fact of geography and a fact of history. It will neither go away in space nor in time. Treating Pakistan as a permanent enemy is the best guarantee of their continuing to remain one. The wiser long-term course is some accommodation which would make Pakistan less life-threatening.

That can only come through dialogue, not bombs. We rendered ourselves vulnerable to the Pak N-bomb the minute the BJP leapt into Pokhran-II. For Chagai was written into Pokhran-II. And so was the Musharraf doctrine, published in the papers on 5 January 2000, that Pakistan will use the bomb the day it feels its national security is threatened. That could be when the next mountain goat clears its throat.

There is no alternative to dialogue. We can start today or twelve months down the line. That is a matter of timing. The atmospherics are against any imminent resumption of the dialogue because of Kargil and the hijack. But if we make the Musharraf take-over the reason for postponing the dialogue till the coup d'etat is undone, we would have to wait a long time, a long, long time indeed. Moreover, we would be storing up yet another disappointment for ourselves since no civilian government has proved any easier to deal with than the many military governments of Pakistan. Chasing the will o' the wisp of democracy in Pakistan is not, and should not be, an Indian problem. How we conduct the dialogue, and not with whom, is the crux of the matter. If it is to be Musharraf, so be it.

To not hold bilateral dialogue would be to invite multi-lateral intervention. For a quarter of a century, it was the Simla Agreement, with its premise and promise of bilaterally resolving outstanding issues between our two countries, including the vexed issues relating to Jammu & Kashmir, which inured the India-Pakistan relationship from overt outside intervention, even when nothing much was happening on the bilateral front. Pokhran-II changed all that. For it paved the way to Chagai. And thus the overt emergence of two nuclear weapon

powers on the subcontinent. Tension between the two countries, particularly over Kashmir, is being played up globally and
the region is being dubbed the most dangerous nuclear flash-
point in the world. We can and must puncture this motivated
pretension, but if we refuse to talk to Pakistan, tensions can only
increase, not decrease. And since nuclear war is everybody's war,
the absence of bilateral dialogue would give the perfect opening
for third-party interference. For the present, the international
community, in particular the US, is content to say that if India
and Pakistan address themselves bilaterally to the resolution of
their differences, the world would be prepared to wait and
watch. But if bilateral dialogue is broken, and tension, therefore
persists, it is doubtful if the world will long wait for our
by-your-leave to plunge once again into the maelstrom of
India-Pakistan relations, as they did to our disadvantage
through the 1950s and 1960s.

There are those, notably the editor of the *Indian Express*,
Shekhar Gupta, who view with equanimity the prospect
of an international settlement of outstanding India-
Pakistan issues, notably J&K. The view has few takers. Indian
distrust of international good offices is well-founded. It is
difficult to imagine that such intervention would be construc-
tive, objective and impartial. Chances are it would be biased in
favour of Pakistan, as in the past. And we no longer have the
Soviet Union to bail us out in the UN Security Council. Yasser
Arafat may be ready to settle for Panchayati Raj in the Gaza
Strip. I cannot see India embracing with any enthusiasm an
Oslo-Washington route to ending disputation over Kashmir or
any other India-Pakistan bilateral issue.

If, therefore, we want matters of the subcontinent to be settled in the subcontinent, we will have to resume our bilateral dialogue with Pakistan sooner rather than later. What, however, is there for India and Pakistan to talk about? Even so staunch an advocate of dialogue with Pakistan as former prime minister Inder Kumar Gujral has asked what there is to talk about when all Musharraf wants to talk about is Kashmir. But which Pakistani leader ever wanted to talk about anything else? It took us twenty-one years from Simla to Narasimha Rao's letter to Benazir of October 1993 to even signal a willingness to talk of 'issues related to J&K'. Six years on, not one meaningful discussion on J&K has been held. Discussions on other matters too have, by and large, come to nought. What, therefore, is there to talk about? And to where would such dialogue lead?

To nothing. To nowhere, is the answer most Indians (and, perhaps, most Pakistanis) would give these two questions. I am not so sure. Clearly, any serious negotiation must begin with each side stating its maximum position. To reveal in advance what might be the areas of compromise would be very bad strategy; to state what one has to state in a spirit of take it or leave it is no dialogue. Settlement has to arise out of dialogue. It is the process which leads to the outcome. If the outcome is known, dialogue is not necessary; if the outcome cannot be different to the starting point, there can be no dialogue.

There are many possible outcomes to a dialogue on J&K. They range from convincing the other side to abject surrender by either party, to the abdication by both sides of their claims, to an internationally-supervised plebiscite, to a joint condominium, to the lopping off of Ladakh and Jammu from the state, to the 'Trieste formula', to the conversion of the LoC into an international border, or any other solution that admits of human ingenuity. Dialogue could also lead to complete stale-mate. But it is not that there is nothing to talk about, or that talking about everything would be acceptable to either or both. The point is to get talking, as sincerely as possible, and see whether dialogue can lead to a conclusion.

We have never given dialogue a chance. It is time we did. Not perhaps tomorrow or within any specific time-frame, but whenever possible and preferably as soon as possible. To puff out our chests and insist there is nothing to talk about but the vacation of aggression in J&K is, of course, tub-thumping patriotism of a most satisfying kind. But is it patriotic to forget that our security forces are being killed by the hundreds in the Valley? Civilians by the thousands are dying. An entire people — the Pandits of Kashmir — have lost their hearth and home. We could put off dialogue by keeping peace in the Valley, as we did from 1972 to 1989. But once the Valley spun out of control, it inevitably became the happy hunting ground of the Pakistanis and now, after the nuclear tests, a focal point of unwelcome international attention. To postpone dialogue indefinitely because we do not like military rule in Pakistan is to invite upon ourselves the very consequences our diplomacy has sought to save us from these fifty-two years.

Suffice it to say that success of a dialogue hinges on so structuring it that it takes place at specific intervals (the more frequent the better, as with the weekly US-North Vietnam Hotel Majestic talks in Paris) and a pre-determined venue (my pref-erence is for the Attari-Wagah border in the manner of Panmunjom, so that no interlocutor has to leave his country to come to the negotiating table). There should be a single principal interlocutor on each side so that the agenda is not fractured and the trade-offs can be inter-sectoral. There must also be a 'zero hour' in which negotiators can get current grouses off their chests before settling down to longer-term business. And the agenda should be open-ended so that either side can bring up what it wants, instead of grounding the dialogue in procedural side-issues, as has happened thus far. Above all, it must be immutably settled, in advance of the commencement of the dialogue, that the dialogue will be uninterrupted and uninterruptable. That is of the essence.

For everything in my experience suggests that it is impossible for Indians and Pakistanis to talk to each other for any length of time without finding common ground. The trouble is we have not talked to each other for half a century, uninterrupted and uninterruptably.

Should we not be doing so in Y2K?

# Navel' Offensive

DANIEL LAK

Though there
is much
cultural sharing
between India
and Pakistan,
there is also
a cultural
partition,
says the BBC
correspondent
in India. Now
if only the two
countries
could confine
their wars to
the media ....

The scene is a sports stadium in a Karachi suburb known more for brutal ethnic violence than rock concerts. Tonight, things are different. A rambunctious crowd of boys and young men is milling around, chain-smoking, laughing loudly and greeting each other with elaborate hugs. Girls huddle in small packs in the stands, modestly dressed in shalwar-kameez, draped with shawls. But this is the boys' moment; testosterone seems to hang thick as mist in the night air. The girls gossip and giggle and are ostentatiously oblivious to male attempts to catch their attention.

Suddenly a wild voice screams from the stage.

'ASALAM ALEKUM!'

The words are chopped, staccato. In the crowd's ecstatic reply, the ancient phrase sounds syncopated, like some mysterious medieval version of reggae.

'WA-LAY-KUM A-SAAA-LAAAAAM!!'

I'm not at a Muslim revivalist gathering aimed at errant youth. Nor is it a mullah bellowing from the stage at the bear pit of blue-jeaned boys and swirling cigarette smoke. It's Ali Azmat, lead singer and dervish-in-chief of Junoon, Pakistan's favourite rock band. This is the first concert in Karachi for Ali and the boys since I got them banned from performing and appearing on television in Pakistan last year. I didn't mean to get them in trouble but given the circumstances, I wasn't surprised that officials in Islamabad reacted with such vehemence. Junoon had committed the ultimate sin in Pakistan: letting the side down on enemy territory.

The band was in India in May of 1998, a momentous time to be anywhere in South Asia. Who could forget the day that the newly-elected BJP Prime Minister Atal Behari Vajpayee made his announcement that India had successfully tested nuclear weapons in the desert west of Delhi. Junoon certainly can't. The group played two concerts in Delhi in the time between the Indian nuclear tests and Pakistan's response. There was very real international pressure on Pakistan not to respond, and Junoon chimed in on the side of restraint by Islamabad.

Salman Ahmed, guitarist and driving force behind the band, led the way as Junoon took the stage that evening in Delhi. The cheering began with the opening notes of *Sayonee*, the number one song in India and Pakistan at the time. From that moment, Delhi belonged to Salman and Ali Azmat. The two Pakistanis danced wildly and kept performing as parts of the stage collapsed in a freak windstorm. The fans, young people as well as families, sang along. They put their arms around each other and swayed in time to the music. They demanded three encores. That's when the trouble began.

I was crouched in front with a camera crew for the closing notes of the final song — *Sayonee* again. We swung around from filming frantic fans to catch the goodbyes from the band. Ali whirled his shaggy mane of hair one more time; Salman played a final, screaming run of notes on his guitar; *Sayonee* ended with a soaring crescendo of sound. 'Good night India. We love you,' the dervish screamed, 'One day we'll all be one again.'

I remember thinking at the time that it was a strange thing for a Pakistani to say in India at the best of times, let alone in the immediate aftermath of the nuclear tests. Suggesting that the two countries might ever become one was a denial of Pakistan's founding principle: that Muslims in South Asia could not live in a unified India.

Junoon played their final show in Delhi the next evening,

*Junoon got into trouble with the Pakistan establishment for
their remarks during a tour of India but have
since been rehabilitated.*

and the television report ran on the BBC World channel all that
day. Salman rang me at midnight, full of enthusiasm, and
brushed aside my concern about any impact of the film in
Pakistan. 'No way, man,' I remember him saying, 'the message
is getting through. Peace, love, music — no war, no weapons,
no worries.' How wrong he was. Junoon returned to find even
their fans a bit bemused by the excitement they had generated
in India. A prominent Karachi rock critic, Hasan Zaidi, told me
that there was a growing feeling in the city that the band took
itself a little too seriously, and had been incredibly naïve during
the 1998 tour of India. 'Ever since they started this "Sufi thing,"
we wondered about them,' Zaidi said, 'They're a rock band and
a damn good one, but it's only music and we all have to watch
ourselves as far as India is concerned.'

Then a letter arrived in Salman Ahmed's postbox several weeks after Junoon returned to Karachi. It was from the Ministry of Culture, and its stiff, bureaucratic tone is equally familiar to people on both sides of the border. One of the many things that India and Pakistan share is a humourless, seemingly parasitic bureaucracy that treats the populace with sniffy disdain and contempt: a holdover from British colonial times, according to many.

The letter said the group had questioned the legitimacy of Pakistan while in India, that they had spoken against the country's nuclear policy. It ordered Salman Ahmed and Ali Azmat — interestingly not bassist and American citizen Brian O'Connell — to 'appear before the below-mentioned joint secretary to explain said remarks, broadcast by BBC and Star TV'.

It wasn't the first time that Junoon had fallen afoul of the government. State-run Pakistan television was already prohibited from broadcasting their concerts, or even mentioning their existence. This was supposedly because of their Western ways — long hair, blue jeans and apparent rock stars' lifestyle. In reality, the ban was politically motivated. The then prime minister, Nawaz Sharif, didn't appreciate any sort of criticism or opposition, certainly not from a rock band that sang about 'inquilab'· (revolution) or accountability. Junoon had also helped ex-cricketer and anti-corruption campaigner Imran Khan raise money for his cancer hospital in Lahore. But there had been no hint of treason charges in any of the band's previous conflicts with the authorities. This time, it was serious.

Eventually, they got everything back, in spades. Junoon's political comeback began well before Nawaz Sharif lost his job so dramatically in October of 1999. The band members helped their case by playing a concert to honour the 'martyrs' of the Kargil conflict, despite the fact that Pakistan is still coy about admitting the loss of any regular soldiers in the fighting with India in the hills of Kashmir in the summer of 1999. Salman Ahmed angrily denies wry bazaar rumours in Karachi that his group's connections to Gen. Pervez Musharraf have anything to do with its return to acceptability. Asim Raza, who directs Junoon's videos, is related to the general on his mother's side.

It was fascinating watching the rehabilitated Junoon perform in that suburban stadium in Karachi. The band brimmed with confidence onstage, despite a shaky sound system. The fans were hardcore 'Junoonis' — the word means 'crazy' in Urdu. They leapt and whirled and danced long into the night. The boys tore their shirts off and spun around in circles until they collapsed from dizziness. Standing in large sweaty groups, they took turns hurling each other into the air. If I had been at a concert in the West, alcohol or drugs might have explained such behaviour. But these young, largely middle-class Pakistanis were completely sober. They were getting carried away by the music and the sheer joy of letting themselves go in public. When I interrupted the party to ask some questions, they showed a surprising sense of national pride and support for the military coup.

'We're Junoonis man, proud Pakistanis, Pakistan Zindabad! Musharraf Zindabad!' screamed seventeen-year-old Bashir Amir. Later, as he rested, leaning against the stadium wall, he told me, 'Look at us. We're the young generation here. We've got the best rock and roll. In India all they have is that horrible

**239**

movie music from Bollywood.' He broke into a gyrating dance routine, reminiscent of an Indian film, hips thrusting in a grotesque parody of sexual intercourse.

As he said, there is a certain amount of pride in Pakistan about the relatively tiny pop culture scene. The success of Junoon in India and abroad has generated much of that pride, but there's also a lot of interest in the careers of artists of Pakistani-descent who do well in foreign lands like Britain or even Norway. It seems to be the classic case of a small country feeling dwarfed by a larger neighbour looking long and hard for examples of success beyond the borders of home. As a Canadian, it's an attitude that is familiar to me. My fellow countrymen and women have been looking anxiously south of the border at the US for decades now. I put this to cultural commentators in Karachi, people like Hasan Zaidi. Was Pakistan really producing something that was different and better from what was coming out of India?

'Look, India has A. R. Rehman and Anu Malik, but they write film music. They don't have anyone like Junoon that's really big abroad, that can combine styles and appeal to people every-where. We've got other groups like that; people will hear about them soon. And we're open to their (Indian) stuff too.' He named two pop stars from India. 'We like Sukhbir Singh and Daler Mehdi, but quite naturally, we prefer our own success stories.'

The view in India is quite different, of course. Popular culture, as driven by the dream machine of the Mumbai film world, is so powerful that it can absorb influences from all over. Junoon, to many in India, was just another rock group that caught the public mood at a certain time. Similarly, few Indians attached much significance to the popularity in their own country of Pakistani soap operas.

Wondering then if pop culture had any role at all to play in breaking down barriers and resolving old hostilities, I asked Zaidi if Junoon was right that their message of love and cross-border peace fell on receptive ears, whatever the official reaction in Pakistan. He was sceptical. 'Look at the controversy about them. That showed that we have a long way to go. Our bureaucrats and politicians caused the trouble in the first place but I think the Indian media played it up, first because it seemed that Junoon was being treacherous, then because it made us look like Muslim fanatics. They seem to find that image particularly compelling. We are a weird place with a lot of stupid, contradictory ideas but we're just struggling to make our way like anyone else.'

Like many people I met in Karachi, Zaidi found coverage of Pakistan on Indian satellite television channels disappointing and occasionally jingoistic. 'If pop culture was going to bring us together, we'd have sorted our differences through Star and Zee TV. We all watch it, and they know we do. But they don't seem to make an effort to understand us. That just makes things between us worse.' Karachi bristles with satellite dishes. Soap operas, chat shows and quiz programmes from India are the staple diet in every living room.

Even Indian news programmes are watched eagerly, perhaps because a young, uncertain and still developing national culture needs desperately to know what others think of them. Again the Canadian-American example comes to mind, and I daresay my own experiences with people in India watching the BBC and CNN almost wanting to be offended, but being most distressed of all at being ignored.

**241**

'There's no question that their (Indian) culture is popular here, but so much of what we see emphasises the differences between us,' says Imran Aslam, a playwright and senior editor of the *News*. 'We've grown apart in many subtle ways since Partition.' He admits that deep down, there are immense similarities but recent history has spawned a sort of deliberate and thus unnatural cultural partition. 'I like to say that we in Pakistan are the willing victims of Madhuri Dixit's navel offensive,' he jokes.

'This image of the failed Islamic state is popular in India,' Aslam says, 'I don't believe that they think about us as much as we think of them, but they do have very set views. And they find the contradictions of Pakistan very challenging to those views.'

The proof might lie in the fact that Indian movies like *Border, Dil Se* or *Sarfarosh* that glorify the Indian army and portray Pakistanis as terrorists or fanatics are widely available in Karachi. A film like *Hindustan ki Kasam*, about an assassination attempt on a Pakistani prime minister during a trip to India, is also popular. Pakistanis watch such movies eagerly, and seem prepared to accept the fact that they're being portrayed as wicked Islamic fundamentalists and supporters of cross-border militancy.

Aslam laughs when he tells one story. 'During the Kargil business, there was an unofficial ban on *Border* and that sort of movie. But it wasn't the government. Indian films are technically illegal anyway. It was the video parlour owners' association. They were banning something that was already illegal, and to top it off, they pirate the videos anyway. Patriotism and piracy — that's us writ large.'

No one competes with the Pakistanis when it comes to cynical self-deprecation. As a people, they're deeply aware of the failures and shortcomings of their national experience. And they react with humour, occasional hope mingled with despair and a stubborn sense of pride that they're still around as a country. That may be why they are able to take parallel attitudes towards what they see from India on their TVs; amusement and entertainment from the warmongering films of Bollywood and annoyance at the relentless and repetitive portrayal of their state as a pariah-in-the-making by Indian television. Aslam, born in Chennai, raised in Dhaka, now a confirmed Karachiite, thinks he detects a severe shortage of a sense of humour among media commentators and opinion-makers in India. He says this contributes to the Indian media's tendency to always look for chinks in the cultural armour of a visiting Pakistani.

'I was in Delhi to appear on an episode of the BBC Question Time India programme,' he says, 'and I knew I had to watch what I said. All the other panellists and the compere were just waiting for me to be controversial. To get myself in trouble like Junoon. They thought they had me at the end of the programme. I was asked if I was in favour of the reunification of India and Pakistan. I got them, though. I said "Yes" and they all looked smug. But then I said only if the new country is called Pakistan and is a Muslim state.'

It isn't hard to understand why Pakistanis should feel that the Indian media is hostile to them, and not a peacemaker or a builder of bridges over troubled waters (Most Indians feel the same way towards Pakistani media, particularly PTV, which, they feel, revels in vicious anti-India propaganda). When I was last in Pakistan, everyone mentioned the now infamous row over the affair of the 'grandfatherly peck.' That bizarre

episode began when the elderly and respected writer, Khushwant Singh, greeted the daughter of the Pakistani high commissioner in Delhi with a chaste kiss on the cheek. Singh later
described the kiss as an innocent peck, something a grandfather
might offer his grandchild. The greeting was snapped by a
photographer and appeared in the newspapers of both countries to little or no immediate reaction. Several days later, Indian
newspapers reported that the high commissioner, Ashraf Jehangir Qazi, was in deep trouble for allowing his unmarried daughter to be kissed in public. The suggestion was that wild-eyed
mullahs in Pakistan were furious and wanted the affable and
worldly Qazi's head on a platter. Nothing could have been
further from the truth.

Khushwant Singh now refuses to talk about the affair, and
so does the high commissioner. But what is known is that just

*Pakistan was cool about Khushwant's 'grandfatherly peck' but
the Indian media indulged in a mocking agenda-driven
coverage of the country anyway.*

one Urdu language tabloid, of very low repute, reported alleged criticism of the kiss. That was picked up by an Indian news agency stringer in Islamabad and a round of mocking, agenda-driven press coverage of Pakistan ensued. Pakistanis shook their heads ruefully over the affair. The fact that there had been no criticism of the high commissioner or his daughter from the government, clergy or common man was all but forgotten.

People in Pakistan became aware of the cheek-pecking row through the Internet. On both sides of the border, World Wide Web editions of leading newspapers are read by those with Internet connections. Pakistanis did some mocking of their own when the government in Delhi blocked access to the web edition of the Karachi newspaper, *Dawn*, during the conflict in Kargil.

'They (the Indian government) probably thought Indians would get bored and fall asleep, and then Pakistan would take over the whole country,' jokes Aslam, loyal to a fault to his own paper, the *News*. A common joke amongst *Dawn*'s rivals is that the newspaper is so impartial, so reluctant to take an editorial stand, that it frequently errs on the side of dullness.

We read all the time about how the Web is breaking down borders, challenging sovereignty and making nation-states obsolete. Bill Gates and other Internet preachers say the new e-commerce world has no place for national, ethnic or communal rivalries and former enemies will unite around the notion of making money and surfing the Web. I'm afraid the evidence proves the opposite in the case of India and Pakistan. The middle classes in both countries are embracing information technology and the successes in Silicon

Valley of non-resident Indians and Pakistanis are the stuff of modern legend. But ask around and you hear more stories of Web warfare than softening attitudes and peace mongering. A young woman in Karachi told me of a virtual assault that she experienced during the fighting in Kargil.

'I was in a chat room meant for South Asians. Mostly it was flirting, talk about music and movies and innocent stuff. I happened to mention, in passing, that I was from Pakistan and everyone, and I mean everyone, turned on me.' Her eyes get hard with anger as she tells the story. 'The same people that I'd been chatting to about Usha Uthup or Imran Khan started calling me a terrorist and a warmonger. They demanded that I withdraw my troops. My troops? At that point, we didn't even know for sure in Pakistan that our real soldiers had invaded Kargil. It felt like rape because you get quite close to people in those chat rooms. I haven't been back to that site since then, and I doubt I ever will go back.'

Hacking, deliberate sabotage of websites and data bases, is another regional speciality. The most famous example in recent memory is a successful foray into an Indian Army site on Kashmir by Karachi-based hackers. There is a lot of pro-Pakistan Kashmiri propaganda on the Web, mostly put there by Kashmiri immigrants in Britain and North America. The Indian Army wanted to counter some of that by giving details of its own efforts in the troubled Himalayan state. It was a surprisingly professional effort, not heavy-handed at all, and quicker with information than some army spokesmen in Delhi.

But it ended in grief when the boys from Karachi hacked in. They posted a huge slogan saying 'Azaadi' (freedom), in the middle of the home page. They replaced the words 'terrorist' and 'militant' in the text with 'mujahideen' and 'martyr'. They generally created mayhem and the army had to shut down and redesign the site over a period of several weeks. So much for cyber psy-ops.

That particular group of hackers is almost certainly associated with the Pakistani political party, Jamaat-e-Islami. Like the BJP (Bharatiya Janata Party) in India, Jamaat tends to attract support from educated, urban sophisticates of a natural conservative bent. The new South Asian IT elite is among that crowd. Imran Aslam says Jamaat-e-Islami and technology are old friends. 'During the last Pakistani general election, some bright boy from the Jamaat got hold of a low power television transmitter and put it in a van. They drove around Karachi, transmitting political messages on the same frequency as PTV. You'd be watching cricket, or a music programme, and suddenly the Jamaat leader was on the screen, begging for your vote. It was the first opposition political advert in the history of Pakistan.'

It's clear that Aslam has a grudging admiration for the techno-whiz kids of Jamaat-e-Islami, even though his own politics couldn't be further from their professed version of Islamic democracy. 'A friend rang me up from Germany,' he said, 'I had done some media consultancy work for his company. They wanted to break into online gambling, the Internet casino business and they needed the software. I was trying to be funny so I suggested the Jamaat boys to him. The joke was on me. Not only did they bid for the contract, they got it and designed some of the best gambling software my friend's company had ever seen.' Aslam laughed, 'I suppose they'll use the profits to spread the word or maybe just do some gambling.'

I got a sense of the cultural conflicts and cul de sacs of this peculiar region on a trip to Pakistan in November of 1999 — my first visit to that country since coming to India nearly three years earlier. During my time in Delhi, I had come to see Pakistan through the prism of Indian perceptions and concerns. Like many Indians, I saw the country next door as a source of cross-border violence in Kashmir, a place that one might blame for mysterious explosions and separatist insurgencies, a failed state tottering on the brink of Islamic anarchy. If you had asked me for an assessment of Pakistan a few years ago, when I was based in Islamabad for the BBC, I would have been much more positive and optimistic. Perhaps my judgement at that time was clouded by the many close Pakistani friends I had made. Was it possible to live in India and be anything other than hostile or a hardliner towards Pakistan? It was a question that needed an answer. That's why I had to go there again, to explore that faded sense of optimism and examine Indian-generated perceptions with a journalist's sceptical eye. And that's why I travelled by road and rail from Delhi to Islamabad.

The bus from Lahore to Islamabad used to take more than six hours with at least one near-death experience along the way. But this section of the British-built Grand Trunk Road from Calcutta to the North West Frontier has now been replaced by a superb European-style motorway. 'Nawaz Sharif's Taj Mahal' was how one acquaintance in Lahore described it. Our luxury coach hurtled through the night at a stunning 140 kilometres per hour, on a divided highway. The journey was trouble-free; no brushes with disaster while passing on a blind curve; no buffalo carts looming suddenly in the beam of the headlights; no drunken or drug-addled truck drivers lurching all over the road. There's nothing quite like it anywhere in South Asia. I could have been on an autobahn in Germany or an American interstate highway. Except for one thing, the video entertainment on the coach was pure Bollywood. Not only that, it was the latest, hottest film from the young director, Ram Gopal Verma, whose work seems based on Hollywood's ultra-hip Quentin Tarentino in its use of violence and wickedly funny language. The film, *Shool*, was released in India in 1999 and is, of course, technically illegal in Pakistan. Enemy propaganda perhaps, part of a subtle cultural undermining of the ideology of Pakistan maybe, but it sure captivated my companions on the bus. They were especially fascinated by the actress in the lead role, Raveena Tandon, whose revealing costumes in the film opened another of Imran Aslam's new 'navel fronts' in the ongoing cultural battle.

My search for renewed optimism about Pakistan was largely in vain but I did find many things to challenge the distorted and ideological view of the country acquired during my time in India. Pakistanis remain warm and hospitable to a fault. Most, even devout Muslims, deplore Islamic extremism. They have a wicked sense of humour, especially about politicians and the elite. Those who can afford it enjoy a tipple of the prohibited alcohol whenever they can. An Arabic-speaking journalist friend in Islamabad, glass in hand, explained it to me this way. 'You see, at the time of our Holy Prophet, there was a lot drunkenness and wife-beating going on. The Arab tribes were drinking rough spirit made from dates, so when the Koran speaks about not taking alcohol, that's what it's referring to. There's no mention of gin and tonic,' he said, draining his glass and calling for another.

I renewed many such old acquaintances and, yes, enjoyed a few gin and tonics with my Muslim hosts and friends. But I also found an undercurrent of fear and uncertainty, and a hardening of attitudes about India. 'It's those nuclear tests,' a prominent Islamabad architect told me, 'and the BJP types. They play into the hands of our extremists and I think it suits their view of Pakistan. Rather than encourage the liberals, they fan the fundamentalist flames to justify their own behaviour. A lot of the violence against non-Muslims here is in response to problems in India.'

There is an element of truth in that assertion. I remember the aftermath of the demolition of the Babri mosque in Ayodhya in 1992. Pakistanis, glued to their television screens and radios, followed the progress across north India of bands of Hindu fanatics and BJP ideologues on the so-called 'Rath Yatra', a journey in motor vehicles decorated like chariots from Hindu mythology. It was a cynical and dangerous exercise aimed at rallying popular feeling behind the Hindu revivalist agenda of the BJP and it resulted in the razing of the mosque and thousands of casualties, especially among Indian Muslims. On the day the ancient building was torn down, Pakistan was, at first, silent. Then the reports began to come in of attacks on the tiny Pakistani Hindu community. I soon lost count of the number of temples destroyed — hundreds probably, many little more than an altar in peoples' homes. Dozens of Pakistani Hindus died, completely defenceless against enraged mobs led by extremists and opportunists calling themselves Islamic leaders. It was a ghastly mirror image of the situation in India. Never has a country lost the moral high ground as quickly as Pakistan did in the wake of the Babri mosque episode.

I did find — on subsequent journeys around the country
to see the destruction — a few points of light in an overwhel-
mingly dark picture. Many Muslims told me privately that they
deplored the attacks on their Hindu neighbours. In the tiny
settlement of Mithi, deep in the Thar desert in southwestern
Pakistan, local Muslim businessmen helped their Hindu
colleagues stop an attack on a temple by local activists of
Jamaat-e-Islami. I still remember Mohammed Iqbal, a Muslim
shoe shop owner and head of the local Chamber of Commerce,
pointing to a gun leaning in the corner of his shop and making
a grim promise. 'Anyone who comes to bother a Hindu here will
face that. I'll kill them if I have to. Even Muslims.'

It was the Ayodhya crisis and its aftermath that made me
realise that India and Pakistan are interdependent in a paradoxical, sometimes brutal way. Their faults and foibles mirror each
other, and self-serving, corrupt elites use the bogie of the evil
neighbour to compensate for their own failures. All the cultural
sharing in the world hasn't changed that. The Indians who went
to Lahore in February of 1999 for the Indian prime minister's
historic bus journey across the border could be seen weeping
with emotion in the streets of the old capital of undivided
Punjab. They hugged taxi drivers and amused their hosts with
the latest gossip from the Mumbai film world. They gorged on
kebabs and Lahore's famous lentil dish, sat ki dal. They basked
in the acute thrill of discovering the familiar on enemy soil.

Yet a few months later, the two countries were at each
others' throats, on the brink of a nuclear war over a Pakistani
military incursion into Indian Kashmir. There are strong
suggestions that solutions to many of the fifty-year-old cross-
border disputes had been in the works before the fighting in
Kargil — a realpolitik-style settlement motivated by the soaring

cost of defence in both countries, the need to free up resources for development and stimulate the economy of the entire region. What happened? Why did such momentum come to naught?

A widely held belief in Pakistan is that powerful vested interests on both sides of a hostile border want to keep the situation tense for their own purposes. 'We've got our military and civil establishment; they've got their own version,' a friend in Lahore told me, asking to remain anonymous. 'Don't be fooled by any of this cross-border confidence-building stuff or any of the cultural diplomacy. It's all window dressing. We do it to keep the Americans happy. There are so many people who profit from hostility, like businessmen that don't have to compete with more efficient traders from the other country, arms dealers and all of the so-called national security "hawks". Here it's the army that would lose from peace; over there, it's another bunch. They control us like puppets. I wouldn't be surprised if they had regular meetings for strategy sessions.' My friend, I believe, is wrong. But he's not alone, at least in Pakistan, in believing that hostilities are deliberately maintained and manipulated.

After Karachi, Islamabad and finally Lahore again, it was almost time for me to go home. But there was another call to make — to a woman described by a Western journalist who is a frequent visitor to Pakistan as 'South Asia's Nelson Mandela'. Asma Jehangir is a prominent human rights lawyer and a founder of the independent Human Rights Commission of Pakistan. She exudes goodness, energy and humour. I have rarely met anyone with such personal strength, except perhaps her sister and law partner, Hina Jilani. Asma arrived at my hotel in Lahore to pick me up, accompanied by a hulking policeman with an AK-47 submachine gun. 'More death threats,' she explained blithely, waving her cigarette at the armed guard. Her tireless work for women, non-Muslims and children in Pakistan has earned her many enemies. Her husband, a Lahore industrialist, has been driven to the brink of bankruptcy several times by governments and Islamic groups stung by Asma's vigorous campaigns.

Her view of what's going wrong in Pakistan would be music to the ears of many in India. 'We armed and trained the Taliban, if not now then during the Afghan war, and sooner or later, they'll come marching into Pakistan. It's probably inevitable. Our relations with India are distorted and endangered by the situation in Kashmir, for which I blame both countries. Our elites steal and plunder and ignore the plight of the vast majority of the population and even liberal politicians use extremists and criminals as their shock troops. We pay the price in crime, in sectarian violence and in our economic mess.'

One thing Asma won't do is utter words like those in public in India. Like so many other campaigners who will stand up to almost anything in Pakistan for the sake of her principles, she's wary of the Indian media and establishment. She knows that her criticisms of her own country will be used to reinforce the Indian notion that Pakistan is a failed state and Partition must be acknowledged as a massive mistake. So in India, she keeps her concerns about Pakistan to herself and speaks in general about human rights. Asma says it's time to move on from Partition and the sterile debate over whether Mohammed Ali Jinnah was right or wrong when he founded Pakistan.

'It's too late to worry about things like that. We have two

countries here with huge problems and so many opportunities to work together to make things better. Instead, we go around sniping at each other at every possible opportunity and we lose out. We're not seen as grown-up by the rest of the world, not able to take care of our problems ourselves. That has to change.'

I asked Asma why she did it; why she kept fighting for humane and sensible things in a world and a region that seems to be going increasingly mad. Many other people would give you a misty eyed speech about duty, or God, or something equally lofty. Not Asma. She squints at you through a haze of cigarette smoke and says, 'I don't know. I must be crazy or something.' It is refreshing and depressing at the same time to talk to people like Asma Jehangir. However horrible the implications, they tell it like is, yet they also inspire hope with their candour and humanity. They are pillars of the society that could be if this region ever gets its act together. I am still not sure whether my travels through Lahore, Islamabad and Karachi were a success or not. I still think that Pakistan is a deeply troubled place that causes immense regional instability with its activities in Kashmir, it's knee-jerk anti-India policies. Equally, India demonises Pakistan at every opportunity and seems to delight in its largely self-inflicted problems. India seems to need Pakistan as a distorted image of how things can go wrong. Any notion that India would benefit greatly from a stable, more secular economically prosperous neighbour is swept away with bouts of media-driven glee over just how bad things are across the border in the 'failed state'.

An Indian friend who writes for a leading newspaper in Delhi once told me: 'To hell with Pakistan. I'd be happy if we could just forget about them, let them succeed or fail on their own, and just worry about ourselves, our own problems. But we have them to blame, to compare ourselves to and it makes us feel unjustifiably better that we're in much better shape. They hurt our feelings when they turned their backs on us at Partition and we seem determined never to let them lose sight of that. It's a waste of time and energy to keep living in the past.'

Imran Aslam's parting words to me in Karachi were largely similar. 'Things are changing all around us. Both our countries are highly centralised and bureaucratic in structure, anarchic and ever more free in practice. We're both banging away in the software and e-commerce world. We're sharing what we want to share through smuggling and piracy and ignoring official prohibitions. Even if we fight our wars in the media, that's better than on the battlefields of Kashmir or Punjab. I'm not really optimistic that the official position of both countries will ever change. But the people matter more. And we, the ordinary people, middle classes and business community, are going to be global citizens a lot sooner than our politicians, bureaucrats, or even generals. Then there's no stopping us.'

Even if he is talking about the Islamist entrepreneur-hackers of Karachi, I hope he's right.

# The Indus Person

## AITZAZ AHSAN

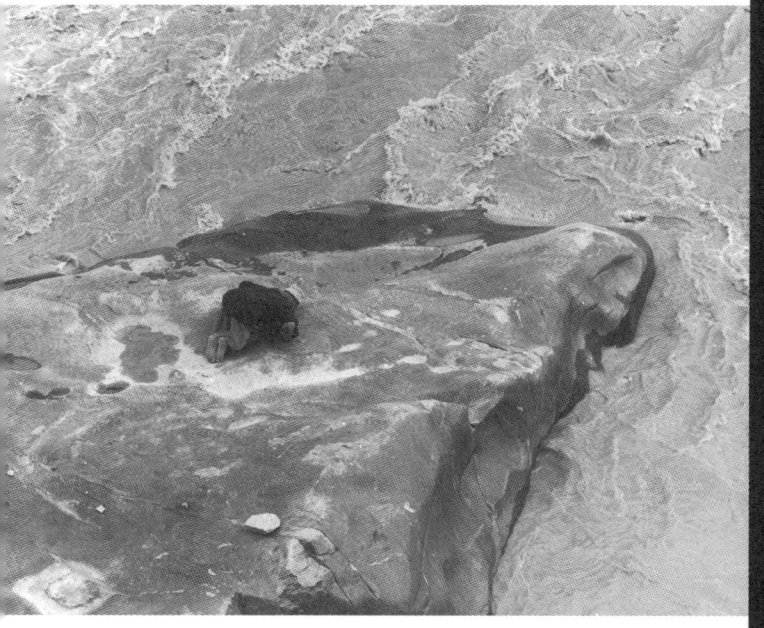

The Indus (Pakistani) man has always been different from his Indian counterpart, because the history of the two regions has been distinct and separate, argues the Lahore-based lawyer-politician.

The personality of the Indus person (the present-day Pakistani) and his most prominent attributes have been shaped by his history. This is, by and large, a history distinct and separate from the history of India.

This latter statement may shock some but it is true.

The exclusive, almost jealous protection afforded by the sky-scraping mountain ranges and the stormy tropical coastline appear to have quarantined the subcontinent like a continental island. It displays a rare compactness, albeit on a continental scale. It appears to be a remarkable and exceptionally unified fortress. High and forbidding mountain ranges seem to protect its north and northwestern frontiers. The deep expanse of the Indian Ocean becomes a vast intercontinental moat on all other sides. With its endless succession of mountains, plains, plateaus, and rain-soaked coastal strips, it seems one vast unity, a single, natural, indivisible whole.

From the Pamirs in the north to Cape Comorin in the south, from Gwadar in the west to Assam in the east, and from the Arabian Sea to the Bay of Bengal, the Indian subcontinent has always been treated by the geographer and the historian alike as one single unit.

Yet this is not so. Indus and India have always been distinct and separate.

Indus (Pakistan) has a rich and glorious cultural heritage of its own. This is a distinct heritage, of a separate nation. During the last six thousand years it has, indeed, remained separate from India for almost 5,500 years. Only the three 'Universal States' (of the Mauryans, the Mughals, and the British), welded these two regions together in single empires. And the aggregate period of this compaction was not more than five hundred years.

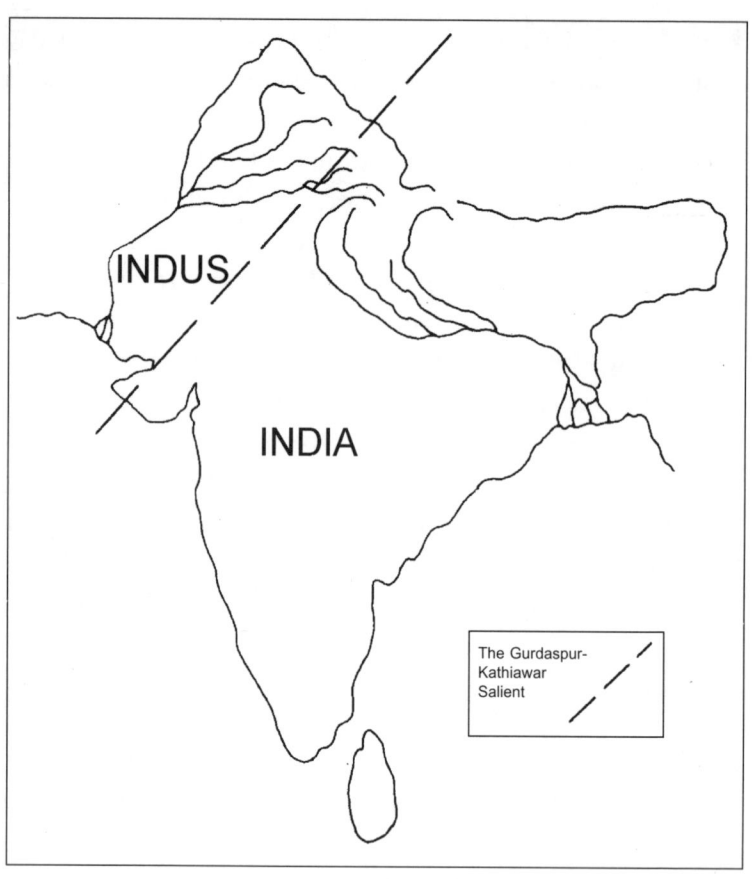

INDUS

INDIA

The Gurdaspur-
Kathiawar
Salient

For the remainder, from prehistory to the nineteenth century, Indus has been Pakistan. The year 1947 was only a reassertion of that reality. It was the re-emergence of a primordial federation. As such, 'Pakistan' preceded even the advent of Islam in the subcontinent.

What has to be perceived is that more than the giant mountain ranges that separate the Indus region from Central Asia, that indiscernible hump between Indus and India along a line roughly connecting Gurdaspur in eastern Punjab to Kathiawar on the Arabian Sea has been the critical dividing line of history and culture between two lands, two peoples, two civilisations: Indus and India. This 'Gurdaspur-Kathiawar salient' approximates the border that today exists between India and Pakistan, thus giving to it the sanction and strength of history.

It is to the north, along this line, that the Ganges comes closest to Indus' southern-most tributary, the Sutlej. But, as if in keeping with the character of the two civilisations and like water draining off the opposite sides of a sloping roof, each journeys away to drain out in the opposite direction. The sources of both the rivers are within a hundred miles of each other. But their divergent courses take them to their deltas almost fifteen hundred miles apart.

This has also been the case with the civilisations that have flowered on the banks of these two mighty streams. They came close to each other in some periods of history. Each took stock of the other, and then each went along its own individual, distinct, and opposite way. It is significant that the only politically noteworthy attempt to fuse these two civilisations took root in the area of the vital watershed itself, the virtual 'no-man's-land' between the two streams of water and civilisations: eastern Punjab and Sindh. Here, a culture drawing both from Indus and India could be developed. Thus, Guru Nanak was able to establish a durable order on the eastern tributaries of India. And the soil also nurtured the Sufi strains of an outstanding Islamic movement.

Without explicitly mentioning this divide, ancient prehistoric scriptures testify to the primordial distinctiveness of the two regions. Thus while the Vedas belonged predominantly to the Age of Bronze and also to that of the tribes and the nomadic cattle-breeders and were cast under a strong Central Asian influence, the epics (Mahabharata and Ramayana) belonged not only to the Age of Iron but also to that of caste, to the surplus-producing shudra, the sacrifice-oriented Brahmin, the Jumna, and the Gangetic plains. The Vedas belonged to the Indus. The Epics were composed in India. In many ways, they too represented the differences between Indus and India.

Though the Indus region was held by the Gangetic region in the Mauryan period, it was soon taken over by the Bactrian Greeks — who merged it with the vast territory they held on either side of the river Oxus that spans most of modern-day Uzbekistan, Tajikistan, and northern Afghanistan. There it then remained under succeeding dynasties for an unbroken period of more than five hundred years. This alone is longer than the span of the Mauryan, Mughal, and British empires put together. Finally, with the crumbling of the Kushan state, the Guptas pulled Indus, for another brief interlude, towards the Ganges.

In the centuries that the Indus suffered successive invasions (those of Alexander, Seleucus, the Mauryans, the Bactrians, the Scythians, the Kushans), India witnessed an era of relative peace and quiet, a peculiar gift of isolation. It enabled India to devote itself to the progress of science and philosophy. But despite these intellectual advancements it ousted Buddhism from its borders. Indus then became a Buddhist sanctuary for several centuries. The soft strains of non-violent and pacifist Buddhism were akin to the latter-day teachings of the ascetic Sufi saints of Islam — the transition from Buddhism to Sufism was thus easy.

In some uncertain interregnums, the fortunes of Indus did fluctuate between Central Asia and India. Such fluctuations, however, were never without resistance on the part of Indus states and peoples. They stoically but actively resisted the pull of both sides. It is because of this resistance that the periods of Indus' independence were always much longer than the periods of its annexation by one side or the other.

There is no doubt that there is a large area of cultural commonality between the people of Indus and India. They have after all coexisted through the length of time. But the Indus person has also interacted, in this extended period, with the Central Asian and Persian (though not with the Arab) regions and peoples — and these influences have also shaped him and given him his distinctiveness.

As we shall see, invasions and resistance over centuries made the Indus person a natural and brave soldier. But the anarchy that often accompanied the invasions denuded him of common civic values and of the urge to save, reducing him to a compulsive consumerist with little respect for rules and with no skill of administration. While the British Raj gave him administrative institutions as well as laws, and while it greatly enhanced his soldiering, it did little to inculcate in him the skills of administration. Instead it laid in him the basis for an 'urge to overtake' irrespective of merit.

But the frequent incidence of invasion imbued him with other traits too, many of a lesser order. So frequent indeed has been the incidence of war — the invader frequently being repulsed and the victor often winning by a quirk of fortune — that the Indus person has been given to the belief that battles are not necessarily won by the superiority of science and technology, but by those who are righteous. Righteousness is with the faithful, even though they may lack technology, and scientifically more effective strategies. His role model remains the man on horseback, brandishing a sword and charging at the enemy, single-handedly killing a hundred armed opponents.

Having been subjected to abject anarchy for centuries, the Indus person is quite an indifferent administrator. Except for the brief British interlude he has only seen the law being subject to the will of the administrator. Not the converse. He thus sees little need to abide by the rules himself. As an administrator, therefore, he likes to bask in the importance of his office, seeking to exercise arbitrary authority. In fact, the extent of this authority appears to him to be directly proportionate to his ability to abuse it. An officer who cannot bypass all rules to help a supplicant or a friend commands little respect. So all-pervading is this attitude that even the best army officers, steeped in discipline and respect for rules, easily forget what they have learnt when placed in charge of the civilian administration.

The Arabs gave the Indus person his faith, but Persia and Central Asia gave him the Islamic values that were tailored to the needs of the family as distinct from the dictates of a patriarchal tribe. This made him well-suited, above all, to utilise the gift of the Indus river system. Mercifully, the five tributaries of the Indus had gifted agriculture to the Indus person. He had thereby graduated from a primitive, patriarchal tribesman to a devoted family man in a softly matriarchal environment.

The Indus person has acquired some of the most essential attributes of his faith and beliefs due to the physical location and geography of the Indus region. He may be loathe to admit this reality but the fact is that even in receiving and adopting Islam and its values the Indus person took more from Persia than from Arabia.

In socioeconomic and cultural terms, the nomadic Arabs were not an agrarian community. The prospects of agriculture were almost nonexistent in the thirsty and inhospitable sands of the deserts of the Saudi Peninsula. The Arabs remained a pastoral society, leading camels and goats from one oasis to another in search of the scarce foliage upon their lands.

Besides being nomadic, the Arabs were also a patriarchal society. Women were not only denied inheritance, but the girl-child, considered a shameful liability, was often buried alive at birth by the pre-Islamic Arabs. Only the male could fight the many internecine and intertribal wars that became unavoidable in a search for an occupation of the scarce green patches and oases in the desert. The male member of the tribe was its supreme asset.

The Indus civilisation, on the other hand, had on it the distinct imprints of a matriarchal society, many features of which continue to enrich it to this day. Indus cities were supported by an agrarian base from the time of the prehistoric Mohenjo-Daro civilisation. There were settled villages, producing a surplus of agricultural products. Agriculture compels man to settle down on or near his fields and landholding. It binds the erstwhile nomad to a fixed abode where, in due course of time, a house, and then a colony of houses (village or city) comes up. The hutment, the house and the village settlement impels the dissolution of the tribe and the evolution of the family.

The environment of the family gives to the character of the Indus person a certain civilised softness. Bonds between the members of a family are strong. Responsibility and care for ageing parents and grandparents, for instance, is a normal trait of the Indus family. There is no abandonment, even in times of economic stress and penury. Even in the interpretation and application of the Sharia, Indus remains largely the land of the Sufi. Only in the arid and backward areas of the Indus region do nomadism, the tribe and the patriarch survive.

Moulded by the ancient traditions of the family, the Indus woman is intelligent, brave, and confident, and has initiative. No amount of fundamentalist mumbo-jumbo can obscure these features of her character. The fact that she continues to be subjugated has more to do with economic reasons common to most underdeveloped countries. But even when she is put behind the veil, she remains the social driving force, giving impetus and direction to the son and the husband. Denied education and opportunities of gainful employment, she is the greatest untapped resource of Indus and of Pakistan.

Indus citizens have repeatedly and consistently rejected intolerant fundamentalism. This has been attested to in each one of the elections held since 1937. This does not, however, imply that the Indus person is irreligious. In fact, the crowds at the shrines of his saints show that he is deeply religious. But he shuns fundamentalism. He readily gives his soul to an unorthodox Sufi but resists the influence of the dogmatic and inflexible maulvi. Though there has been a spillover effect of Afghanistan in Pakistan recently, the underlying cultural values of a majority of Pakistanis have not been affected.

Fundamentalism and sectarianism in their contemporary violent and intolerant form survive only at the fringes of Indus society, despite an entire decade of recent state patronage. The Indus person stands at a distance from fractious sectarian movements, quite apprehensive about their potential for violence and conflict. He has, however, not yet reached the stage where he can actively craft and participate in pacifist movements that seek to bring about tolerance and harmonious coexistence between the various faiths and sects in Pakistan.

The cosmic battles of the Vedas were fought by Indus men heroically resisting, with a combination of courage and guile, the invasions by unending waves of the Aryans. By Chandragupta's time Indus was well initiated in the art of resistance. It was, therefore, only natural that Chandragupta picked up those vital lessons of guerilla warfare and martial traditions that were to win him an empire. It was in this region that Poros finally put an end to Alexander's further advance and ambitions. As none other than Taimur blazed a trail of fire, pestilence and death, all the way to Delhi and back, it was an Indus chieftain, Sheikha Gakkar, who displayed the audacity to attempt to block, both ways, the march of that 'Scourge of the

Earth'. The Delhi sultan, Muhammad Tughlaq, spent the last four years of his life in a luckless and frustrating campaign in Sindh. Babar himself made three unsuccessful attempts to cross the Indus to Delhi, and succeeded only in his fourth attempt. It was again a lion-hearted and vigorous young Abdullah Bhatti who managed to pin down the emperor for almost a decade in the Punjab.

A hundred years later, Khushal Khan, a soldier and a poet, set up an independent state in the Khattak territory on the banks of the Indus and resisted Mughal might with full vigour and valour. In more recent times, the ferocious Nadir Shah and the hardy Ahmed Shah had to face immense resistance in the Indus region. The British too had to fight many fierce battles despite their technological superiority, before they could annexe Indus to their Indian empire.

When drilled, trained and subjected to discipline the Indus person makes an excellent military officer. During a century of service in the British Indian Army, and as the critical factor in countless successful assaults in the most difficult and alien terrains all over the world, with his own life often hanging in the balance, the Indus soldier seems to have developed many sterling qualities. He has learnt the advantage, in peace and war, of obedience to superior officers. This quality also makes the Indus person an industrious and untiring workman under a watchful eye or when supervised by an efficient administrative system.

The Indus person had seen the most blood and blazing wheat-fields in the eighteenth century. Like the eleventh, this was the century of expeditionaries. The death of Aurangzeb and the constant fratricidal intrigues and wars amongst his successors had sapped the empire of all its energy. And Indus with its hardy tribesmen and peasants and its brave warriors stood in the way of expeditionaries peering through the narrow mountain passes to its northwest.

Each Persian and Afghan campaign was vigorous but of short duration. The invaders were content with collecting revenue and booty, and then returning to their homelands across the mountains. What perspective the Indus person had of such campaigns of Central Asian expeditionaries has best been described by F. S. Aijazuddin, who sees them 'stripping every place they entered until there was nothing left to flay when they discarded it, denuded of all vestiges of wealth, property or civic order.' They thus left several lasting imprints upon the Indus psyche. What was the purpose of saving when pillaging armies were going to take everything? The attitude is reflected in the idiomatic refrain 'Khada peeta layay da; Baqi Ahmed Shahay da' (Only that which you eat [or consume] is yours; The rest will be appropriated by Ahmed Shah).

To this day, the Indus people, as a race, are willing to spend rather than save. And they do so ostentatiously, as it is not considered a flaw, but a virtue of sorts. They will even borrow to overspend at marriages and betrothals.

Another lasting impact has been the minimisation of expectations the people have of their administrators. Historically, there were no permanent administrators, just an endless stream of marauders. The main object of the government was to collect revenue and to expropriate. Citizens had to be coerced into submission and then fleeced. This raised the threshold of tolerance that the Indus elite displayed towards oppressive and cruel rulers.

The Raj re-emphasised the Indus-India divide. Under the Raj, the development of the canal system, the opening up of much of the Indus region through railways and roads, and particularly the policy of 'colonisation' of lands that accompanied these advances, had two long-term effects: it left a lasting imprint upon the psyche of the Indus person, and it extenuated the Indus-India divide.

Before the modern canal system, much of the Indus region was shrubland, called 'baar'. Even today, such names as Neelibaar and Gondalbaar, signify the areas lying away from the riverbanks, between the rivers Sutlej, Ravi, Chenab and Jhelum. Many other areas were desert. Although there was a rich and primordial tradition of agriculture from the times of Mohenjo-Daro, which had given impetus to the development of the family, most of the agriculture was confined to the 'belas' or 'kutchas', areas contiguous to the river banks. Seasonal floods provided the necessary water for crops like wheat, cotton, and sugarcane. The scale of cultivation was necessarily limited but the population was concentrated in these riverine strips.

The British, in seeking to open up more lands to the cultivation of cotton, sugarcane and wheat, found that even the soil under the 'baars' or shrubland was fertile. The deserts also displayed great potential. Only water was required. An enormous network of barrages and canals was therefore planned. Millions of acres came under cultivation. But these had to be actually ploughed and harvested by people. These 'new' lands were 'colonised' and allotted to the local landless or to settlers brought from other lands.

The allotment of lands was a windfall for the Indus populace. Thousands of peasant families were moved from distant villages to the new lands in the nineteenth and twentieth centuries. In some areas, such as Sargodha and Jhang, large tracts were gifted. In others, such as Sahiwal and Faisalabad, smaller parcels were given out. Overnight, the fortunes of the families changed: landless peasants became landowners, and robber-barons became landlords. If the district collector, or even his assistant, was pleased with an aspirant, the largesse of the state suddenly descended upon the beneficiary. Those who had collaborated in the wars against the Punjab and Delhi were, of course, not to be forgotten. They got the lion's share and became the new, economically powerful ruling class. Collaboration and submission had their rewards.

This was not a ruling class born out of a struggle. It was not a ruling class that had won its place through wars or sacrifice as in Europe and America. On the contrary, it had obtained its position of pre-eminence by doing just the opposite. But the end justified the means. The 'success ethic' became the principal social norm of Indus society. It laid the basis of the 'get-rich-overnight-irrespective-of-merit' syndrome, which was to be consolidated later.

The construction of canals and railroads was, however, crucial to the imperial exploitation of Indus and India. Henceforth, England would develop with Indus and Indian wealth, and would use her developed methods to suppress and subjugate more South Asians, both Hindus and Muslims.

At the time the Indus was being 'agrarianised', India saw the rapid development of commerce, industry and the bourgeoisie. The early spread of bourgeois development amongst Indians (predominantly Hindus) also increased the divide between India and Indus. All industrial centres were in India, none in Indus. Indus remained backwardly feudal. The nationalist movement also broke out first in the bourgeoise-dominated areas in India. By the late nineteenth century, the Indian bourgeoisie, fully matured, wished to break the bonds of its partnership with the British and to undertake the struggle to replace the British merchant, manufacturer, and government. Indus was, as yet, far behind.

The primary distinction, therefore, that coincided substantially with the Hindu-Muslim divide was that the Hindu (i.e. predominantly Indian) society had a vigorous bourgeoisie while the Muslim (predominantly Indus) society was still agriculture-based and feudal. The two communities were in different historical time-zones. Even if this divide had not coincided with the religious divergence, it may perhaps still have been grave enough to impel a division of the subcontinent. The feudal and agrarian Indus society would have in any case been repelled by the prospect of becoming subject to bourgeois India. As a Muslim majority region the deprivation was more deeply felt.

Since status and wealth were acquired easily overnight, they had to be displayed to make the world aware that the newcomer had 'arrived'. A repetition of the 'rags-to-riches' scenario confirmed and consolidated in the Indus person the traits of consumerism and ostentation.

In the first decade after independence, people with bogus settlement claims were able to obtain properties left behind in Pakistan by Hindus and Sikhs who evacuated to India. Often, there was no merit in the allotment process. The penniless vagrant managed to get 'evacuee' industrial units, big bungalows, well-placed shops and markets, cinemas, and agricultural land. Thousands of those who actually deserved this 'compensation' for lands, houses, and estates that they had had to abandon in India upon their migration to Pakistan were denied their rights and became paupers. The patronage of the 'settlement' officials was capricious and arbitrary. Whomsoever the officials and fortune smiled upon became rich overnight, and then began to establish and advertise their new-found social status through an ostentatious display of wealth.

The 1960s brought in a new manner of becoming rich, another 'fortune by lottery'. It was the decade of Field Marshal Ayub Khan and of his desire to create a distinct constituency for himself. It created a new elite at the lower level by the introduction of what was called 'basic democracy'. Members of the local bodies became the all-powerful electorate of the nation. They had not begun with that prospect when they were first elected. They were invested with this privilege by a single presidential order. Overnight, they gained unprecedented political and social importance. Soon they were translating this newly-acquired political clout into economic wellbeing.

This was also the decade that introduced a new and arbitrary method of distribution of the spoils of the state: the 'Permit System'. The sanction of the state in the shape of written authorisations called permits was required for all manner of economic and commercial activity. These permits themselves had a market value and could be, and were often, sold. There is the story of the governor who gave his favourite civil servant two permits for textile mills: one to sell to raise the funds to put up the textile mill sanctioned by the second permit! The brother of the new textile tycoon, on the other hand, remained a member of the lower middle class. Fortune was as arbitrary as the governor. The Indus person could see that merit played no role in the advancement of one brother and the failure of the other.

Most of the patronage was, undoubtedly, showered upon the Indus elite of (West) Pakistan. They were allotted permits to set up industries. Even those who set up initial industries in East Pakistan reinvested their profits in West Pakistan. They built their houses in Karachi and Islamabad; they kept their liquid assets headquartered in Karachi; they put up further industrial units in Faisalabad and Karachi. With profits earned in East Pakistan, they bought agricultural lands in Sindh and Punjab; and they sought and obtained bank loans, duty concessions, and protection from competition through the ban on imports. These industrial houses grew and learnt to thrive in a greenhouse environment. The growth of the Indus capitalist was, thus, as artificial as the growth of the Indus feudal.

The predominant trend was so powerful that the latter-day West Pakistan-East Pakistan rift and the creation of Bangladesh out of East Pakistan was also a result of it. Bengal had always been very much a part of Gangetic India and the world of maritime trade and commerce. Its bourgeoisie was also more mature and sensitive, quite distinct from the landlocked and landowning elite-turned-bourgeoisie of the northwest. It saw through the comprador style of the Indus bourgeoisie. The divide of 1971 was therefore not prevented by commonality of religion. The divergence of social and political culture was more powerful and irresistible. When this inherent cultural distinctiveness outpaced the commonality of religion, many were utterly confused. Their 'Two-Nation Theory', adverting only to the Hindu-Muslim divide on the basis of religion, appeared to have come to naught.

The 1970s was the global decade of oil power. After the six-day Arab-Israeli war, the Arab world began to use the 'oil weapon'. It brought development for the Arabs — cities, highways, refineries, seaports and airports had to be constructed. Labour was required for these tasks and hundreds of thousands of Pakistanis obtained jobs in the Gulf states. Another divide was thus created by what many have called the 'Dubai syndrome'. It could perhaps be described better as the 'lottery syndrome'. Neither merit nor competence really counted. The brother who was able to find employment in the Gulf states became rich; the one who could not remained poor. Overnight, another new class with economic power was created. What kind of labour the one abroad was employed in was immaterial. It only mattered that he had made it in the world. He and his family had become rich 'overnight'.

The 1980s brought the curse of heroin. The Afghan war was perhaps partly funded by the drug trade. Anyone who made a 'successful' trip through customs returned rich. He could build a plaza of shops and offices in elite markets and his children were able to go to the best schools. The one who hesitated, or was infirm of purpose, lost the round. By this time, nobody asked how their rich new neighbour had acquired his wealth. Nobody sympathised with the honourable one. This collapse of values legitimised corruption as a social phenomenon.

The 1990s have exposed persons in high positions dipping into the till and reserves of nationalised banks and cooperative societies to amass wealth and to multiply their assets. 'Lottery culture' and the impulse to get rich overnight were thus perpetuated. Unlike in Europe and India, the economically dominant classes of Indus have not attained ascendancy and established their 'right' to dominate through any historic struggle, or through perseverance, restraint, prudence, thrift savings or wise investments.

To conclude, the Indus person has been shaped by various influences and factors including the river Indus and its tributaries, the aboriginal matriarchalism, the introduction of iron and agriculture, the disintegration of the tribe and the emergence of the family, the Sufi saints, the anarchy of four hundred years, and the goals pursued by an alien imperial power during a century of rule over him and his lands. These have made him what he is: a devout member of a family unit, a person who is not won over by the fundamentalist but who is a brave soldier though a bad administrator. He is not given to savings and is a consumerist with little civic sense. Yet he is an industrious person who has a progressive and liberal outlook.

# Notes on Contributors

KHALED AHMED has been consulting editor at the *Friday Times*, Lahore, since 1993. He was also editor of the Urdu weekly, *Aajkal* and the *Frontier Post*, Lahore. He was earlier joint editor of *The Nation*, Lahore. He has also been third secretary in the Pakistan Foreign Service and was posted to Moscow and Prague.

AITZAZ AHSAN is a member of the Senate of Pakistan and an advocate in the Supreme Court there. He has held various portfolios as a minister in the Pakistan government (1988-93) as well as in the provincial government of Punjab (1976-77). He served several terms as a political prisoner, and without trial, during the martial law imposed by Gen. Zia ul-Haq. He has also written a popular cultural history of the Indus region, *The Indus Saga and the Making of Pakistan.*

MANI SHANKAR AIYAR, educated at Doon School, St. Stephen's and Cambridge, was India's first consul-general in Karachi (1978-82). Since then he has been a frequent visitor to Pakistan, and accompanied late prime minister Rajiv Gandhi on his three visits to that country. In 1994, he published his *Pakistan Papers*. He is at present secretary, All India Congress Committee, but the views expressed in his essay are strictly personal to him.

Born in Lahore in 1943, TARIQ ALI came to study politics and philosophy at Oxford University in 1963 and became the first

Pakistani president of the Oxford Union. His opposition to the military dictatorship in Pakistan prevented his return to his own country and he became an unwilling exile in Britain. His first books (over a dozen) were works of history, politics and biography, which were translated into many languages. In 1990 he began to write fiction and has written four novels — *Redemption, Shadows of the Pomegranate Tree, Fear of Mirrors* and *The Book of Saladin*. His new novel, *The Stone Woman*, will be published in June 2000. Tariq Ali has also written screenplays as well as plays for stage and television. He is an editor of the *New Left Review*.

JASON BURKE was born in 1970 in London and graduated from Oxford University in 1992. He worked for the *Sunday Times*, London for five years before moving to the *Observer*. He was the *Observer*'s South Asia correspondent in Islamabad until January 2000 and is now with the paper in London.

PAMELA CONSTABLE is the South Asia bureau chief for the *Washington Post*. A full-time journalist for the past twenty-five years, she has reported from more than twenty countries, including Chile, Haiti, Cuba, Russia, South Korea, the Philippines and El Salvador. Before joining the Post in 1994 to cover immigration and Hispanic issues, she was a Latin American correspondent, diplomatic reporter and Washington editor for the *Boston Globe*. She previously worked for the *Baltimore Sun*. She is the co-author of *A Nation of Enemies: Chile Under Pinochet* (1991).

DANIEL LAK was born and raised in Canada. He worked in Canadian radio and television before joining the BBC in 1987.

After a few years in London, he resigned to travel through Asia and the Pacific. In 1992, after rejoining the BBC, he was appointed its Islamabad correspondent. He was posted to New Delhi in 1997.

SHAHID-UR-REHMAN is correspondent of *Kyodo News* of Japan in Pakistan and also strings for *Asiaweek, Business Week* and *Nucleonics Week*. He has been covering Pakistani politics, economy and diplomacy for nearly three decades. In 1980, he was awarded a fellowhip by World Press Institute, Minnesota and in 1995 was invited by the Washington-based Wisconsin project to assist in the preparation of a special report on Pakistan's nuclear programme. He has written two books — *Who Owns Pakistan?* and *Long Road to Chagai* (a history of Pakistan's nuclear programme).

Born in Hyderabad in Andhra Pradesh, AZIZ SIDDIQUI has been editor of *Gulf News*, Dubai; *The Frontier Post*, Peshawar; and *The Pakistan Times*, Lahore and Islamabad. He has taught mass communication at Punjab University. He is currently joint director of the non-government Human Rights Commission of Pakistan, and contributes to newspapers, including a weekly column in *Dawn*.

SANKARSHAN THAKUR was born in Patna (Bihar) in 1962. He went to St. Xavier's School, Patna, and Hindu College at the University of Delhi. He began his journalistic career with *Sunday* magazine in 1984 and joined the Delhi bureau of the *Telegraph* in 1985. He is currently associate editor of the paper.

S. AKBAR ZAIDI was formerly associate professor at the Applied Economics Research Centre at the University of Karachi, where he taught for fifteen years. He has written four books on Pakistan's political economy, and conducts research and undertakes consulting assignments occasionally. He writes frequently for the Pakistani and international press.